# The Modern American Frugal Housewife Book #4

## Emergency Prepping

I0455383

### Jill b.

Copyright © 2016 Jill b.

All rights reserved.

ISBN: 1530111943
ISBN-13: 978-1530111947

# CONTENTS

# 1 Introduction

Peaceful terror.

The snow kept falling. The temperature was far below zero. The power was out for days. Our taps were dry. Many roads were shut down. We had nowhere to go.

We had just moved into our new home in Colorado from New Mexico and were now trapped in our home, under six feet of snow. We were city folk now trust into more extreme country living. We knew no one - not that it mattered since large portions of the state were at a standstill. We were totally unprepared with no food other than what we had on hand; no water, electricity or even proper winter attire in one of Colorado's worst blizzards in recent history.

This book is not an ultimate survival prepper guide. If you're looking to prep for the end of the world, a permanent world economic collapse, a zombie apocalypse or talking apes taking over the world, this book is not it. There are many outdoor survival books on the market written by outdoors men and women or by battle-hardened soldiers that cater to the above scenarios.

This book is not meant to be a catch-all book but rather, a starting point for you to think about how you might want to prepare for a bug-in situation. I discuss some topics of importance in-depth while other topics are better discussed in great detail in books of their own.

Some tips and ideas may be useful to you while others may not. I was born and raised in an apartment in a tropical big city but have lived in the Northeast, suburbs of the high desert in the Southwest, a mountain town in the high altitude mountains (9,000 ft) of Colorado and currently homestead in the rural hills of almost-subtropical Southern Oregon.

I've seen much of the world but I'm not a super ninja warrior nor thankfully, have I experienced war or unrest. I am a wife and mother, battle-hardened only by my experiences. My experiences will shape this book, which I have written for the concerned frugal housewife and/or mother in mind. It is a book for women and to a lesser extent men, who are interested in prepping for smaller emergencies that creep up unexpectedly. Emergencies like natural disasters which can result in a grid-down situation, or long term unemployment or underemployment. Because the topic of prepping is so vast, I will focus on bug-in prep.

Ten years ago, I would never have thought about prepping. In fact, the notion was so foreign that it never crossed my mind. My husband and I were both born and raised in large cities and always took the city infrastructure for granted.

Our experience during and after the blizzard quickly taught us to be preppers. Thankfully, even though we were ill-prepared, we had a wood stove and wood, enough food, and some candles to get us through. We have been preppers ever since, adding to our self-reliance cache for almost a decade now.

Remember that prepping is also a state of mind. Without it, all will be lost, regardless of what you have on hand. In this book, I will do my best to cover what we can do to prep ourselves in as frugal of a way as possible.

## 2 THE NECESSITIES

In our modern American frugal housewife scenario, I will assume a bugging-in situation where we have shelter and air quality remains safe. I also try to consider city, suburb and rural living conditions in each prep. Some these ideas may also be applied to prepping your bug out location.

According to Maslow's hierarchy of needs, our physiological needs forms the largest, most fundamental level of needs. Physiological needs are needs that are essential to our survival. That is air, water, food and shelter.

### Buckets and More

Water is the most important item that you need to store. But before we put the cart before the horse, we need something to store the water, as well as many other items in - buckets. Stock up on plastic buckets with lids. Not only can you store water and food in them, they are very useful for other activities including but not limited to, washing laundry, gardening and waste collection. They stack easily and do not take up too much space.

Plastic buckets come in a range of sizes but 3-5 gallon buckets are generally the most useful. You can normally get them, with lids for free at grocery store bakeries. Depending on where you live, they might not be easy to get but keep asking for them when you go grocery shopping. Otherwise, you can purchase them from big-box stores like Walmart or from hardware stores like Home Depot for about $2 each. I will refer to using these plastic buckets throughout this book.

As you slowly integrate your prepping into your daily life, you may also find that you'll need tools for the kitchen, gardening, cutting wood and knife-sharpening. I've included a list of other tools that you might need in the Appendix to help you get started.

# 3 WATER

Now that we have our containers taken care of, we can discuss water. Some parts of the country are blessed with abundant water resources. Others are not. Some areas may suffer from hard-to-reach, polluted, or inconsistent water supplies. When we lived in cities, clean, portable water just flowed from the tap. You didn't have to think twice about it.

However, thinking about our water supply became more of a forethought when we had to draw water from our own well. The water flowed -- as long as we had electricity to work the pump. In snow-ins when the power went out, the water went with it.

Whether you live in the city or in the country, it is important as an emergency prepper to consider possible worst case scenarios. What if government and/or city services are disrupted? What if the water supply becomes contaminated whether from natural or man-made disasters, or from acts of terrorism? Where will you get your water? Again, the answer will depend on your location and living situation.

For some, drilling a well is a viable option. For others, collecting rainwater is a good idea (but not a good idea in states like Colorado where collecting rainwater is illegal). If you live near the coast, a simple desalination setup might be practical. In our part of rural Oregon, wells yield poor quality and quantity. Collecting rainwater is viable in winter but not so much in summer, when it only rains occasionally. However, collecting surface spring water is a very good option in our case.

You can never store too much water. Storing water is more important than food. Even in modern history, it is one thing that many people in a war-torn regions fail to store. Without water, you are left with grains and dehydrated foods that you can consume very little of. We too were figuratively caught with our pants down when we were snowed in for days. In our case, we were lucky to be able to harvest water by collecting fresh snow, running it through a filter and then boiling it.

Do not use water from spas, hot tubs, swimming pools, toilet flush tanks or bowls, water beds or radiators. In most areas where pollution is not a problem, you can collect fresh snow or rain. You can use river or lake water as long as it has not been contaminated by everyday pollution or by natural disasters like floods. Make sure to test and disinfect well water after a flood.

Never use water that has debris or smells or looks questionable. It is generally better to use flowing water than still, stagnant water. Regardless of the water source, it should be treated. If the water is cloudy, allow it to settle before filtering it through a clean cloth, paper towel or coffee filter.

According to the EPA, the water should then be brought to a rolling boil for at least a minute or for at least 3 minutes at altitudes above 5,000 feet. Allow the water to cool naturally and store it in clean, covered containers. Boiling will kill most pathogens but will not remove other contaminants like heavy metals.

Where possible, it's best to store as much portable water as you can before disaster strikes. Here's an approximate amount of water that a very water-conservative household needs:

Washing dishes by hand with contained water: 10 gallons
Washing a load of laundry by hand with a mobile washer: 10 gallons
Bathing with a container of water: 1 gallon for an adult or 1/2 gallon for a child
Composting toilet: 0 gallons

According to the Department of Homeland Security, one person needs one gallon of water per day for drinking and sanitation. Nursing mothers, children and the sick will need to be more water. If you have pets, livestock or a garden, you'll need more water. In very hot weather, you may need to double the expected rations. The Homeland Security recommends that you have at least a three days' worth of supplies on hand but if you have the room, it's best to aim to store at least 52 gallons per person as a starting point.

## Water Storage

Unfortunately, if you live in an apartment, your storage options are the most limited. An obvious choice to water storage is to have enough bottled water on hand. As a frugal housewife, you can you can occasionally get for packs of bottled water for free at Staples. Refer to SlickDeals (http://slickdeals.net) to keep track of deals. If you'd like more information on getting items free or cheaply at Staples, please refer to "The Modern American Frugal Housewife Book #3 - Moms Edition" (http://byjillb.com).

During an emergency, your water heater tank is a good place to retrieve water from. If you have enough space, you can add an extra backup by storing water in food-grade covered buckets or in food-safe 55 gallon drums. You can sometimes find second hand drums for as low as $5 each on Craigslist (http://craigslist.org). Buy only drums that have been used to store food, preferably a food that is easy to clean out, like juice rather than cooking oil. Some bulk food retailers or wholesalers may also be willing to give their used drums away for free.

You can also consider purchasing a water bladder storage unit like a Water Bob (http://www.waterbob.com), which currently costs about $25, and can hold about 100 gallons of water. Fill it up if you expect an emergency to happen. You never know when your water supply will stop during an emergency. Other places to stash water bottles include behind and/or under furniture.

If you live in a home that sits on some property, your ability to store water increases. Storage options include storing water jugs to storage tanks, cisterns, ponds, pools and even elevated gravity-fed tanks. Your budget and space constraints will determine what storage options will be practical for you. For most people, storing water in containers or storage tanks will be the most feasible options, with bucket or container storage being the cheapest option.

You can use plastic drinking bottles that have been washed and cleaned, as long is they're not made from thin plastic.

Avoid saving milk jugs because the milk proteins tend to adhere to the plastic, even after washing.

If possible, use plastics labeled with 2 (which is preferable) or 5 recycling numbers, which are considered food-safe. Plastics with a 1 recycle number are one-time use food-safe plastic. If you're using buckets to store your water, bear the weight of filled buckets in mind, especially if you're stacking them. A full 5-gallon pail will weigh a little over 40 lbs. I suggest storing water in both bottles as well as plastic food buckets. The former will be easier to pack in a bug-out situation and the latter is easier to store and rotate in a bug-in situation.

The containers should preferably be opaque and should be stored in the dark, as sunlight can accelerate algae growth and cause plastics to disintegrate faster. UV rays may also affect the chlorine in the water. The containers should also be sturdy and secure enough to withstand potential disasters like earthquakes and floods.

## Water Preservation

### Chlorine

If you're storing municipal water, it should already have been treated with chlorine and you won't need to treat it further before storage. However, if your water is from an "off-grid" source like a well or spring, then you'll need to add chlorine yourself, which will kill *most* bacteria.

According to the EPA, you should add is 2 drops of **unscented** chlorine bleach (with 8.35% sodium hypochlorite content) that has no additives (like color-fasteners or additional cleaning agents), for every quart/liter of water (or 6 drops of chlorine per gallon of water). One 4-gallon bucket of water will require approximately 1/4 tsp of chlorine.

The water should have a chlorine smell when you open the container. Let the water stand uncovered for 30 minutes before drinking it. If you don't smell the chlorine, add the appropriate amount of chlorine into the container (that is 2 drops for every 2 quarts/liters of water) and allow it to stand, uncovered for an additional 15 minutes before using it. If the chlorine tastes very strong in either case, allow it to stand uncovered for another 2 hours.

The water should be replaced every 6 months. Unfortunately, chlorine itself has a fairly short shelf-life. According to a Clorox Bleach representative, bleach starts to degrade by about 20% per year into salts and water. It should be stored at between 50 to 70F. Chlorine from 6% sodium hypochlorite only has a 3-month shelf-life and needs to be replaced after this time.

## Calcium Hypochlorite

Unlike chlorine, calcium hypochlorite has a much longer shelf-life and is better than bleach for storing water. It is also cheap to use. One pound of granular calcium hypochlorite will treat almost 13,000 gallons of water. You can buy 1lb of calcium hypochlorite for about $10 from various retailers including Amazon and Walmart.

The dry form, also known as "pool shock", is easier to store and has an indefinite shelf-life as compared to the hydrated form. Any "pool shock" you purchase should contain 68-78% calcium hypochlorite and may contain calcium chloride but should not have any additives like water softeners (anti-scaling agents) added.

Add your high-test granular calcium hypochlorite (HTH) only when you are ready to treat your water. Otherwise it will degrade like chlorine bleach, rendering it ineffective over time. **Caution: HTH is a very powerful oxidant so always follow the label for safe handling and storage. Wear eye protection and dilute the calcium hypochlorite in a well-ventilated area.**

The EPA recommends adding one heaping teaspoon (approximately 1/4 ounce) of HTH granular calcium hypochlorite to two gallons of water, stirring until all the particles have dissolved. The resulting mixture is a chlorine solution of approximately 500 mg per liter. **Do not drink this - it is the bleach solution.**

To disinfect water, the EPA further recommends diluting one part of the resulting chlorine solution in 100 parts of water that needs to be treated. The equivalent amount is about 1 pint (16 ounces) of chlorine solution to 12.5 gallons of water. If the chlorine taste is too strong, pour the solution into another clean container and allow it to stand for a few hours before using.

Store your calcium hypochlorite granules in an air-tight container together with the bleach (1 heaping teaspoon to 2 gallons of water) and dilution recipe (1 pint of bleach solution to 12.5 gallons of water).

# 4 Food

Food - a topic that lies close to my heart. Like water, I'm not going to recommend how much of a stockpile you "should" store. That will depend on your budget and more importantly, how much food you can practically store. What I recommend for food storage is to make sure that it doesn't go to waste, which goes against our frugal creed.

There is no reason why you need to keep your food stock separate from regular consumption. In fact, to keep your stock fresh, I recommend constantly rotating your food stock, replenishing it as you consume it over time.

If you have an infant, store some pre-mixed formula. Even if you're breastfeeding now, you may not be able to if you are not properly nourished. Pre-mixed formulas also prevent the problem of not having potable water to mix your formula powder in. You can often get free samples of formula from your pediatrician. Keep your stock fresh by obtaining a few more samples from your doctor but reduce waste by donating your older stock before it expires to a local food bank.

In order to keep morale up and nutrition more well-rounded, it is important to try to stock up on a variety of nutritious food. Good storage foods include canned, dried and cured foods. Frozen foods are a lesser option because of the energy required to keep them preserved. Moreover, frozen food will perish in a grid-down situation. Their shelf-life also tends to be shorter.

# Cans

For the beginner American frugal housewife prepper, start with canned goods. Try to opt for higher quality proteins like canned meat or fish. Certain produce, especially those that retain or increase their nutritional value when cooked or canned, like tomatoes are also good choices to consider.

Canned goods usually last much longer than their imprinted dates. Bear in mind that most dates state "Best by" or "sell by" rather than "rotten by" or "poisonous by". Most foods can be safely consumed 18 months to 5 years past their sell-by date.

Regardless of dates imprinted on the can, always avoid cans that are bloated, rusty or dented, especially if they are dented or rusted around the rims. The canned food should not produce any off-gases or smell bad. Always discard if in doubt.

According to Peggy Van Laanen, EdD, RD, a professor of food and nutrition at Texas A&M University in College Station, Texas, humidity can be a factor in speeding-up deterioration. Keep canned and dry food at 50 to 70 degrees Fahrenheit in a dry, dark place and rotate your food. That is, consume and replace your prepper food stock.

## Canning Your Own Food

Of course, an even cheaper way to accumulate canned food is to can it yourself. Canning home-grown food or food purchased at low prices at the height of the season can go a long way in saving money. Instead of spending money on canned meat, you can easily fill your larder for the price of a hunting or fishing license, or if you do not hunt, you can can at bulk meat prices.

Good places to find canning jars include garage sales and at big box stores like Lowe's and Target after the canning season when they are clearing their supplies out. I avoid shopping at thrift stores because I often find better deals from retail store markdowns or clearances. Your biggest investment will be a water bath or pressure canner, with the pressure canner costing more (about $100-300). If you're lucky, you might be able to snag one at a garage sale for a song.

Things to look out for at garage sales include new canning lids and old canning jars that are half gallon in size (for canning juice only) or smaller and that will fit new lids and rings. Bring screw bands with you to make sure that they will fit. If you are in the market for a canner, make sure that its bottom is not warped and that all the parts are in good working condition, that is they are not rusted etc.

If you've never canned before, there are some basic rules to follow. Low-acid foods like beans, meat and vegetables have to be pressure-canned. High-acid foods like fruit jams and jellies can be water bath-canned. Only follow the <u>most</u> <u>recent</u> recipes by the USDA or University Extension Offices.

Do not change or add ingredients unless the recipe provides instructions on how to substitute ingredients safely. Do not reuse lids unless they are the reusable kind. You can, however, reuse the screw bands as long as they are not dinged, dented or rusted.

If you live in an earthquake-prone area, consider canning in metal cans instead. Again, use only research-backed canning recipes for metal cans. Unfortunately there is not as much information on metal canning available but you can get free metal canning recipes from the University of Alaska (http://hyperurl.co/uafcan).

For more information about home canning, I've compiled a book of canning dos and don'ts, which is for sale at http://byjillb.com. Be safe. My books are a way for me to make a living but if you are on a tight budget, please contact me through my website and I'll email you a free e-book copy.

## Dried Food

Dried food is another excellent storage/prepper option. They tend to have a long shelf-life and need a lot less storage space than other foods. Opt for dried beans and pasta over canned because they generally not only have a longer shelf-life but pound for pound, they are also usually cheaper to buy than their canned counterparts.

Good places to stock up on dried pasta include Costco and Sam's Club. Be sure to check your grocery store's clearance racks as well as they often dump dried pasta at very cheap prices. If you're looking to stock up on dried beans and grains, and if you live close to a more metropolitan area, look for some of your dried beans and spices at ethnic grocery stores which often sell these items at lower prices. Otherwise, your local grocery store or big box store like Walmart are perfectly fine places to stock up on dried goods.

Good times to stock up on your supplies include before Thanksgiving and Christmas, when grocery stores run many loss-leader sales. Loss-leaders sales are sales of items that the stores sell at a loss in order to lure customers in. During the festive season, these usually include baking supplies, canned goods, as well as hams and turkey.

However, grocery stores run loss-leader sales throughout the year. Sales like $10 for 10 are often good times to stock up as well. Using coupons or non-coupon rebates like Checkout51 (http://checkout51.com) will help you save even more. If you are interested in details on how to save at the grocery store, please refer to my other book, "The Modern

American Frugal Housewife Book #1 - Home Economics" (http://byjillb.com).

Grocery stores also normally run deals on beans seasonally-black eyed peas normally go on sale the week before New Year's day, red beans go on sale sometime in February, before Mardi Gras; while pintos and black beans normally go on sale the first week of May for Cinco de Mayo. If they are available in your area, Indian grocery stores may sell lentils (dal), chickpeas/garbanzo beans (chana) and other beans at decent prices.

Look out for 25 lb bags of beans on the lower shelves in the Latino section of most grocery stores. You can also find bulk bean bags at Costco or Sam's Club as well as at Honeyville Grain (http://www.honeyvillegrain.com). However, you will probably do better price-wise buying beans on sale at the grocery store than online.

Don't limit yourself to dried beans, grains and pasta. Most people will not be able to grow their own coffee or teas. Coffee and tea therefore make excellent bartering items in tough times. Other dried foods like dried seaweed and dried mushrooms make good storage foods. They last for years if stored properly in a dark, cool, dry place. Mushrooms provide nutrients including potassium (which helps to regulate heartbeat and lower high blood pressure), selenium (an antioxidant) and niacin (Vitamin B3) while seaweed provides iodine. They do not take up much space, add variety, pack different flavor punches and contain good minerals.

Unfortunately, some of these dried goods are not as easy to find at most stores and are usually fairly expensive to buy. Asian and other ethnic grocery stores are usually a treasure trove of self-stable, varied foods including dried/fermented beans, seafood and meats, which are sold at affordable prices. Store your dried goods in a cool dry place. Properly stored dried beans should last indefinitely, although old beans tend to remain hard (but still edible) after cooking.

If you are storing grains, whole wheat berries separated from the chaff will store longer than ground flour. However, they need to be milled before use and may not always be the most practical choice. If you're stocking up on flour, stock up on white, rather than whole wheat flour. Whole wheat flour contains more oils which are susceptible to going rancid. Similarly, white rice lasts longer than brown.

## Storage

To help to prevent pest infestation, freeze your packages for two days to kill any insect eggs that may already be present in the packages. Store your dried food in their original packaging in your trusty plastic food buckets with gasket lids. If you live in a humid area, add a desiccant.

You can also mix in about 1-2 cups of food grade diatomaceous earth (FGDE) into your 50 lb bags of food (1-2 tsp of FGDE per 1lb of food) to kill bugs naturally. Sprinkle FGDE around the food packages. FGDE is a fossilized hard-shelled algae and is a natural additive that reduces bug infestations by naturally dehydrating them to death. It can also be used to kill garden pests but will also kill beneficials like bees. FGDE is harmless when consumed and *may* be a source of minerals and micro-nutrients. **Note: Be sure to wear a mask during application.** DE is a fine dust and can cause silicosis, a form of lung disease.

Food grade diatomaceous earth is also available in granular form. Use only food grade DE as regular DE may have added toxic chemicals. Most feed and ranch stores should carry FGDE. Otherwise, Custom Milling (http://bit.ly/1wpjwCx) and Perma-Guard (http://bit.ly/1xjm8oi) have food grade diatomaceous earth distributors across the country which will help you to save on shipping.

Bear in mind that plastic containers may not thwart mice. We've had plastic containers that were gnawed through by mice. Unfortunately, the most effective method of deterring mice is the presence of a cat, which may not be a practical solution for some preppers.

## MREs/Dehydrated Food

In addition to dried foods, you may also consider adding Meals Ready to Eat (MREs) to your stockpile. Mountain House and Angson Farms are the main purveyors of more commercially available MREs. However, they tend to be rather spendy so I don't recommend stocking up on to many of these. To help cut costs, you look out for deals at Costco, Sam's Club and Walmart. Both warehouse clubs issue coupons/instant rebates on MREs from time to time so try to wait for coupon deals on these before buying.

Dehydrated food cans, on the other hand, are generally a much better bang for your buck as compared to MREs. I've also found decent prices on Angson Farms #10 cans at Walmart. The shelf-life of these cans is 25 years but Walmart is known to clearance them out. Remember to check the clearance racks before buying as you might be able to score some at 50% off.

If you're unable to find dehydrated food supplies locally, you can also try Emergency Essentials (http://beprepared.com) or The Ready Store (http://www.thereadystore.com/mre). However, most of their items are higher in price and generally have a shorter shelf-life of about 3 years.

On the other hand, The Church of Latter-Day Saints (LDS) (http://hyperurl.co/ldsmre) is a good source for very reasonably priced #10 cans of dehydrated food staples. Certain LDS locations in Utah, Texas, Arizona and Idaho also still operate bulk-food and self-canning facilities. The LDS encourages everyone to be prepared and their facilities are open to non-members as well. Locations without canneries offer ready-packaged items. You can find LDS locations by zip code at http://hyperurl.co/ldscannery.

The best way to save money of course, is to dehydrate your own fruits and vegetables. In "The Modern American Frugal Housewife Book #2 - Organic Gardening" (http://byjillb.com), I highlighted some crops like peppers, potatoes and squash that the modern American frugal housewife can consider growing. However, if you are unable to grow your own produce for any reason, you can also consider dehydrating produce from U-Pick farms, which tends to be cheaper than grocery store produce.

Avoid dehydrating mature squash and other produce because the reconstituted end result will be tough and rubbery. You can also dehydrate lean meats including venison and ham. Just be sure to remove the fat before dehydrating it to prevent the fats from turning rancid. While not poisonous, rancid fats are unpleasant in taste and smell. It may also result in an upset stomach if you eat too much of it, or have a delicate system. Meats that are not dehydrated at at least 140F should first be frozen for 2 days to kill any parasites. The final jerky must be quite hard - much harder than commercial jerky in order for it to last for longer periods of time.

While you can use electric dehydrators, solar versions offer the the best energy cost savings since solar power is free. The most effective solar dehydrators are ones that do not expose the food directly to the sun, which can cause vitamin loss. If you are, or know anyone who is handy, you can even making your own solar dehydrator using plans available at Mother Earth News Magazine (http://hyperurl.co/solardiy).

You can also dehydrate your food in the back of a car on a hot, sunny day with the windows cracked a little for ventilation. The food should be covered with a screen to keep dust and insects away. This is a free or near-free and effective way of solar dehydrating. Remember, that your car will be filled with the scent of the food you were drying so avoid drying any strong or pungent foods using this method.

If you have a wood stove, you can also dehydrate your food by setting your food on a covered screen next to a running stove. Just be sure to rotate the screen to ensure that you don't scorch any pieces and to ensure even drying. I also know of people who've set up a rock bed in the sun and place their drying trays on top of the rocks. The heat radiating from the rocks dries the food in a very cost-effective manner.

I generally avoid buying any dehydrated foods that I can safely dehydrate myself unless it's more cost effective to buy. Good items to purchase include powdered milk, butter, shortening, cheese and eggs, which are difficult to safely dehydrate and powder at home.

If possible, buy powdered full-fat milk which will provide more calories. Powdered milk in a box tends to be cheaper than canned powdered milk. If you live in a humid area however, the canned version might be a better investment for longer storage.

Powdered butter and shortening are best rehydrated with oil rather than water. Substitute the powdered ingredient an equal measurement to the fresh. You may, however need to add a little bit more water or oil in some mixes to produce the right consistency.

Using these powdered ingredients, you can easily make your own homemade cake, brownie, pancake and quick bread mixes at a fraction of the cost of prepackaged boxes. Just add water to the mix before baking. Once opened, these powdered ingredients should last about 5 years if stored in a cool, dry place. Vacuum-sealing or freezing the ingredients will also increase their shelf life.

# Powdered Milk Cottage Cheese

## Ingredients

1. 3 cups powdered milk
2. 6 cups water
3. 1/2 cup distilled white vinegar

## Method

1. Mix the powdered milk in the water until dissolved.
2. In a large enough saucepan, stir the milk on low heat until it becomes hot but not scalding.
3. Slowly stir in the vinegar.
4. The milk should start to curdle.
5. Add vinegar until all the milk becomes curds.
6. Keep stirring with the heat on until the curds separate from the whey.
7. Strain the curds through a clean cheese cloth, saving the whey for baking or to help to start fermentation processes.
8. Rinse the curds in the cheesecloth under cool water and squeeze as much water out as you can.
9. The cottage cheese can be eaten immediately or stored in the fridge for later consumption.

The amount of curds yielded will approximately equal the amount of powdered milk you started with so 3 cups of powdered milk will yield about 3 cups of cottage cheese.

## Condiments

Many condiments also fall under the "dried food" category. Different seasonings can go a long way in helping to prevent appetite fatigue. They provide a whole host of different flavors, even if you're using the same or similar ingredients. I suggest the following seasonings to include in your prep:

1. Garlic powder
2. Onion flakes and/or powder
3. Dried Oregano
4. Cayenne chili powder (which also has many useful medicinal properties)
5. Cinnamon powder, which I buy from Costco
6. Curry powder, which I buy from Asian grocers
7. Pepper, which I buy from Costco

Grow what you can and buy the rest. You get a better bang for your buck if you buy restaurant-sized containers of these herbs and spices. Many herbs and spices also have medicinal properties which may become important in a grid-down situation. In fact, grow many of these herbs will grow in pots, even if you have limited space.

In my book, "Medicinal Herb Gardening for the Homesteading Prepper", I selected and discuss the medicinal plants and herbs are suitable for most climates in the Continental US to add to your prepper arsenal. However, if you can only plant one plant, I highly recommend growing cayenne pepper.

Other spices to store may include mustard seeds, cumin, dried cilantro or any other spice that you use in cooking. Even though they are not technically spices, I also like to have vanilla beans and cocoa powder in my stockpile since I am not able to grow them myself.

Again, be sure to try to rotate your stock as most herbs and spices lose their flavor over time. More "exotic" spices like cinnamon, nutmeg and vanilla beans may also be used as bartering tools in hard times.

## Salt

Salt. Not only does it make food more palatable, salt is essential to life even though the body is unable to produce it. I prefer to use sea salt but storing some easily available iodized salt will go a long way in helping to prevent iodine deficiency in bad times.

Iodine deficiency can give rise to hyperthyroidism, depression and amongst other health problems, preventable mental retardation. Including iodized salt to your prepper food stock is a simple way to add an essential mineral to your diet. If you prefer to store only sea salt; dried seaweed, spinach, mushrooms and ocean fish can also help to supply iodine.

Additionally, salt can be used as a preservative. When salted and dried properly, the shelf-life of many foods can be extended significantly. Bear in mind that using iodized salt can oxidize and darken food, which makes the food less appetizing in taste and appearance. Opt for non-iodized salt if you want to produce more appetizing looking salt-preserved foods. Iodized salt is not recommended for canning. I suggest storing both kinds of salt. Salt can also be used as a mild abrasive for cleaning, and can be used as a bartering tool in catastrophic times.

Sam's Club sells 25 lb bags for less than $5 (the price may vary by location). Look for Morton's All Natural Salt, which is normally used for water softening. Make sure that it is pure salt with **no** additives. If you do not have access to Sam's

Club, try restaurant or food supply stores, or ranch and feed supply stores like Tractor Supply.

The Dollar Store is a good place to buy cheap salt. From time to time, SavingStar (http://savingstar.com) also offers free-after-rebate deals on salt for their weekly deal. If available, simply click the "I Want This" button, purchase the salt from your local grocery store then upload the receipt for a reimbursement. Finally, if you'd like to stock up on bulk gourmet salts, Saltworks (http://saltworks.us) has reasonable prices on exotic salts.

The best way to store salt is to store it in 5 gallon food grade plastic buckets with a gasketed locking lid. Salt is hydroscopic, meaning it readily takes up and retains moisture so you'll need to keep your salt as airtight as possible if you live in a humid area. Aim to store at least 10 lbs of salt per person per year because of its many uses - preserving, fermenting, curing and even cleaning.

## Sweeteners

While not essential to life, sugar is another excellent bartering tool. Abundant and affordable when times are good, sugars like granulated sugar and honey are wise choices to add to your stockpile. Again, the warehouse stores are good places to find bulk sugar bags. However, you might also be able to get better prices pound for pound, when grocery stores run sales on them. Generally, the best time to stock up on sugar is before Thanksgiving, when grocery stores often sell it as a loss leader.

Sugar can not only be used to sweeten foods and help to boost morale, it can also be used as a preservative. Medicinally, "sugardyne", which is honey or sugar mixed with cooking oil in a 3:1 ratio, has been used historically to treat burns, human and insect bites, gunshot wounds and frostbite injuries. However, according to the US Library of Medicine, studies have shown that using honey rather than sugar results in faster, less painful healing.

Sugar should be stored in a dry, airtight container while brown sugar should be stored in a more moist environment. Hardened white sugar can be softened by placing it in a 150 degree F oven for 15 minutes, then breaking it up with a spoon and left in the oven for another hour or so. Brown sugar can be softened using a slice of fresh bread or a dampened paper towel wrapped in plastic wrap; or by keeping an orange peel which has been washed and dried, with the brown sugar.

According to the USDA, as long as your sugars are stored properly, sugar lasts indefinitely while honey will last forever. However, the quality of some sugars like powdered and brown sugars may change over time and are best used within 2 years.

Honey is a wonderful sweetener to keep a stock of. Just be sure that the honey is unadulterated. Unfortunately, a lot of honey, especially if it's from China, is adulterated with other substances including high fructose corn syrup. Look for True Source certified honey (http://www.truesourcehoney.com/) because you cannot always trust the country of origin labelling.

If you can, start your own hive. It's the only way that you'll have a renewable, 100% known honey source. If you're unable to keep your own hives, try purchasing honey from a local beekeeper. If you need help finding a local one, most states have a beekeeper association which you can contact for more information.

Honey should not be stored in the fridge because it will crystallize in colder temperatures. While perfectly safe to consume, you can also return it to its liquid form by placing your container of honey in a bowl of hot, but not boiling, water.

# Oils

Stock up on some oils - you need them. Avoid most vegetable oils as they are generally already rancid (and deodorized), giving them a relatively short shelf-life. Extra virgin olive oil, coconut oil and clarified butter are good options for storage. As long as they are kept away in a dark, cool dry place, unopened containers should last about 2 years.

Your oils should be stored in, or already be in dark glass containers. Do not store your oils in plastic buckets, even if they are food-grade because they tend to not be able to withstand the pressure changes when the oils liquify in warmer temperatures then solidify when it cools down. Also refrain from storing these oils in the refrigerator because the temperature changes from opening and closing the fridge often result in condensation forming in the container, which can cause molding.

In a long-term survival situation, you'll need to harvest animal fats or press oil from oily seeds or nuts for cooking. Walnuts, almonds, hazelnuts, pumpkin seeds and sunflower seeds can all be pressed into oils. Different nuts and seeds will yield different amounts of oil, depending on the oil content of the nut or seed. According to Mother Earth News magazine, to "produce 1 quart of oil, you will need to press 2.9 pounds of walnuts, 3.6 pounds of hazelnuts, 4.6 pounds of peanuts, or 5.3 pounds of canola, pumpkin or sunflower seeds".

If you live in a wine region, you maybe able to obtain free grape seeds to press oil from. If you are pressing seeds like sunflower seeds, use only food-grade seeds and not bird seeds, which may not have the same handling and storage procedure as seeds for human consumption.

Depending on where you live, you might be able to plant Williams Naked Seeded Pumpkin or Peredovik sunflowers for a renewable oil source. Allow the seeds to ripen before harvesting and pre-process them by drying them. To press the oil, you'll need a press which costs around $200 at Bountiful Gardens (http://www.bountifulgardens.org) or Lehman's (http://lehmans.com).

If producing your own seed or nut oils is impractical, then animal fats are a more suitable long-term option. Animal fats that are good for cooking include beef, chicken, pork (lard), duck, goose, bear or wild hog. Even the fish fat under the skin is suitable for cooking but may impart a slightly fishy flavor to your food.

I do not recommend using deer fat which has a low melting point that results in the fat unpleasantly "coating" your tongue and mouth when you eat it. Deer fat can be used for other purposes such as for making soap.

## Rendering Fats

Fats need to be rendered for longer term storage. Some fats like bear fat, goes rancid fast and therefore needs to be rendered quickly. If your raw fat is kept in the fridge, it should keep for about 2 days without rendering. Render your fat outdoors if you want to keep the greasy smell and mess and to a minimum. I however, have always rendered fat indoors.

The frugal housewife wastes little. Separate the fat into two groups: the clean, thick "rendering fat", free of meat, which you can slice into cubes (approx 1/2" each); and fat found in other parts of the animal such as the fat removed from the intestines, or the more gooey fat found between the meat. Everything should be washed well before rendering.

Cut the "rendering fat" into about 1/2" cubes. Heat a heavy bottomed pot (I like using a dutch oven) on low heat. There are two ways of rendering fat - a wet rendering method whereby you add water to about half the total volume of the fat being rendered; and the dry method where the only water added is the water that adhered to the fat during washing. In either method, all the water should evaporate during the rendering process. In the dry method, the fat will be more likely to brown more quickly.

Keep the fat pieces in the pot on low heat, moving them around once in awhile so that they don't stick to the bottom. The oil will eventually ooze out and the pieces of fat will deep fry in their own oil.

Start rendering about a handful of fat, slowly adding more as the first batch renders. In either the wet or dry method, you may see a soupy liquid (water) form. Keep rendering until the liquid evaporates. What's left will be the rendered oil.

The crispy solid bits or cracklings, will eventually float to the top. They should be crispy, not soft and soggy (which means extra rendering is needed). These cracklings can be skimmed off and used like croutons. I think they are delicious but my husband thinks otherwise. Allow the oil to cool and strain it through a clean coffee filter or cheesecloth into a clean, dry glass container.

Next, render the loose pieces of "scrap fat". Depending on the animal, much of this comes from around the intestines. I save time by not cutting these washed pieces up before rendering. This fat produces a decent amount of stock-like liquid which evaporates after a few hours of rendering on low heat. Again, the final products are the oil and cracklings, although these cracklings may have some meat attached to them, resulting in a less crispy product. Using the same procedure as before, strain the cooled liquid oil into a clean glass jar through a coffee filter or a cheesecloth. Save the cracklings for consumption.

The final color of the oil may range from a very light yellow to a light brown, turning white and solid when refrigerated. The oil's color darkens from higher temperatures during rendering, or from any  meat that was left on the fat. Both forms of oil are usable but in the case of pig lard, try to use the light colored oil for baking desserts because it imparts a less meaty flavor. Rendered fat keeps in the freezer for up to a year, often longer.

## Baking Soda

Baking Soda is so useful that it deserves its own chapter in this prepping book because it's cheap, non-toxic and suitable for a great many everyday household uses. As long as baking soda is kept dry and away from odors (which it will absorb), it lasts indefinitely. The cheapest place to buy baking soda that I've found is at Costco, which charges about $5 for a 13.5 lb bag. Otherwise Walmart's 12 lb bags are priced at about $8.

In addition using it as a leavening baking agent, it can be used to deodorize and clean the house, your possessions and your body. Mildly alkaline and gently abrasive with detergent effervescence, baking soda will react with most dirt and grease to form a soap, which in turn helps to remove the grime. It can also be used to absorb, rather than mask odors. In "The Modern American Frugal Housewife Book #1 - Home Economics" (http://byjillb.com), I covered various ways in which you can clean your home with this cheap and non-toxic substance.

However, baking soda has even more uses - it can also be used to put out electrical fires as well as flammable liquid fires from grease, oils, gasoline or solvents. However, it should not be used to put out ordinary fires involving combustibles like wood, paper, cloth or plastics. You can also use baking soda to neutralize battery acid spills by covering the spill with baking soda and washing it away with water as quickly as possible. Baking soda may also be used as an abrasive cleaner by sprinkling equal parts of salt and baking soda on the area before scouring it clean.

While mild, some people may be allergic to baking soda. Always use a small amount to test your sensitivity to it before using it on a larger scale. When applying it to clothes or surfaces, always test it on a small unnoticeable section before applying it to large areas. **Consult a health care professional before using it internally or applying it on broken skin.**

## Antacid

To make a simple antacid, dissolve a level 1/2 tsp in baking soda in 4 oz of water. Baking soda can only be used to neutralize stomach acids. It will not help other stomach problems like gas pain or cramps.

## Skin Irritation Soother

For minor burns, use a paste of 3 Tbsp baking soda to 1 Tbsp water over the affected area and put a wet compress over it. This paste can also be used to relieve poison ivy itching and minor rashes. To soothe insect bites, apply a paste of 1 Tbsp baking soda mixed with 1 tsp water and cover it with a damp dressing.

## Dental Care

Instead of stocking up on toothpaste, you can clean your teeth with baking soda. A solution of 1 tsp of baking soda dissolved in half a glass of water can be used as a mouthwash. You can also brush your teeth by sprinkling baking soda on a moistened toothbrush and brushing your teeth as normal.

## Personal Care

What happens if you run out of soap? Use a solution of 1/2 cup baking soda dissolved in 2 quarts of warm water to wash yourself! To make a simple shampoo, fill a shampoo bottle with 1 part baking soda to 3 parts water. Shake it before applying it to your hair. Rinse with clean water. You can also use baking soda as a deodorant by applying it gently on the underarms.

## Meat Tenderizer

Your local Chinese restaurant probably won't tell you how they process their beef for their stir fries but I will. A lesser known use of baking soda is as a meat tenderizer, which is useful when you need to cook tougher cuts of meat.

Sprinkle baking powder on your sliced meat sparingly. Allow it to marinate in the fridge for half an hour before rinsing the baking powder off thoroughly. Any baking soda that is not rinsed off may bubble when you cook the meat.

Do not apply an excessive amount of baking soda on the meat, which will result in a spongy texture and bitter taste. This meat tenderizing method works best on red meat and works very well in Chinese-style stir fried dishes. There. The secret is out.

Of course, a chapter on baking soda cannot be complete without a section on what baking soda is mainly used for - baking.

## Prepper Cornbread

### Ingredients

1. 1 cup all-purpose flour
2. 1.5 cups yellow cornmeal
3. 1/2 cup buttermilk powder + 1/2 cup water or fresh buttermilk
4. 4 Tbsp egg powder + 1/2 cup water or 2 large eggs, beaten
5. 1 cup water
6. 3/4 tsp baking soda
7. 1 tsp salt
8. 3 Tbsp butter, melted or 3 Tbsp butter powder + 1.5 tsp water

### Method

1. Preheat the oven to 425F.
2. Grease an 8-inch square pan.
3. In a large bowl, combine the dry ingredients.
4. Add the liquid to the dry ingredients, mixing everything until smooth.
5. Pour the batter into the prepared pan.
6. Bake for 25 minutes or until a wooden skewer inserted in the center comes out clean.
7. Serve warm.

## Soda Bread

### Ingredients

1. 4 cups all-purpose flour
2. 1/2 cup buttermilk powder + 1/2 cup cold water or 1/2 cup fresh buttermilk
3. 1/3 cup butter, melted or 1/3 cup butter powder + 3 tsp water
4. 1 cup raisins
5. 1 Tbsp sugar
6. 2 tsp baking soda
7. 1 tsp salt

### Method

1. Preheat the oven to 350F.
2. In a large bowl, combine all the dry ingredients.
3. Stir in the raisins.
4. Add the water and stir until you form a soft dough.
5. If using melted butter, knead it into the dough until smooth.
6. On a greased baking sheet, shape the dough into a loaf.
7. Using a sharp knife, score the loaf 4 times.
8. Bake for 45 minutes or until lightly browned and a wooden skewer inserted in the center comes out clean.
9. Remove from the loaf from the baking sheet and allow it to cool on a cooling rack.
10. Serve warm.

## Buckwheat Pancakes

### Ingredients

1. 1/2 cup all-purpose flour
2. 1/3 cup buckwheat flour
3. 2 Tbsp egg powder + 1/4 cup water or 1 large egg, beaten
4. 1 1/4 cup buttermilk powder + 1 1/4 cup water or 1 1/4 cup fresh buttermilk
5. 3 Tbsp butter powder + 1 tsp water or 3 Tbsp butter, melted
6. 3/4 tsp baking soda
7. 1/4 tsp salt

### Method

1. Preheat a greased pan or griddle.
2. In a large bowl, combine all the dry ingredients.
3. In a separate bowl, mix the wet ingredients.
4. Add the wet ingredients to the dry and stir quickly until smooth.
5. When the pan is hot enough (a drop of batter should bubble when it touches the pan), pour 1/4 cupfuls of batter per pancake onto the pan.
6. When bubbles rise to the top of the batter, and the underside is lightly brown, flip the pancake.
7. Allow the flipped side to lightly brown before removing it from the heat.
8. Repeat the process until all the batter is used up.
9. Serve hot immediately.

# 5 SEEDS

Stocking up on food will help you through a short to medium term grid-down situation. However, in order to keep your pantry stocked long-term, you will need to have survival seeds available. Avoid buying expensive "survival" seed packages, which I feel are purely a marketing ploy on the part of the producers of these seed packages.

Seeds have variable viability and I find some of the guaranteed dates (some as long as 25 years,) hard to believe. These "survival seed" packages also rarely have seeds that are specific to your climate. Do you live in Zone 4 or below? Do you live in the desert, at high altitude or in a tropical area? Your expensive survival seeds probably won't get you very far.

Instead of risking being left with packets of seeds that are no longer viable when you need it most, I recommend starting your own garden and saving your own seeds. Many inexperienced gardeners, my younger-self included, have a naive belief that planting your own food crops are as simple as throwing some seeds in the dirt and watching it grow.

If you do not start practicing gardening today and think that your prepper seeds will save you when your food stash runs out, **you will starve**. Few, if any, first-year gardens, even those planted by experienced gardeners, will be successful enough to feed the gardener. It can take years to figure things out.

We're in our ninth year of homesteading and we're still learning. We've learned from our mistakes. Now that we've moved to a new state, we're spending the first year accessing the local climate and weather and amending the soil before we even start planting.

It's better to buy heirloom seeds or plants from a local nursery because these plants are more acclimatized to your micro climate. Practice growing crops and saving seeds that will grow in *your* region. Your seeds should be open pollinated. Do not buy hybrid seeds for seed-saving because the plants will not grow true to their parent.

Keep your seeds dry and preferably air-locked, away from heat and sunlight. Freezing the seeds will help to extend their viability. Only with experience will you know how much you need to grow to feed your family, what crop works best, how many seeds you need to save for the following year and what yields you can expect from those seeds.

In "The Modern American Frugal Housewife Book #2 - Organic Gardening" (http://byjillb.com), I discussed in detail a few crops that a frugal housewife should consider growing. Generally, good crops to grow include peppers, squashes, potatoes and greens. These crops tend to grow abundantly and are less fickle. You can also preserve these crops in various ways. Avoid planting crops like melons that cannot be easily preserved, in large quantities. Contact your local University Extension Office for recommendations on crops that do best in your climate.

In mild climates your choice of seed crops increases greatly. However, when you live in more harsh climates like

Colorado, where we used to live, it is extremely important to learn the nuances of growing food crops at arid, high altitudes with a short growing season. Not knowing how to care for your precious crop seeds to maturity and not knowing how to save seeds for the next season may mean life and death in dire circumstances.

Don't write this chapter off even if you live in a city apartment! It's important to be able to produce at least some of your own food. Besides container gardening, you can also consider starting a community food garden. Cities have many unused areas like rooftops that are suitable for raised bed gardening. Schools or abandoned city lots are good location possibilities.

If you're trying to be to be more stealthy with your publicly-accessible crops, plant foods that are less easily recognizable as food - that is fruits and vegetables that you don't normally see in your mainstream grocery store.

Learn how to apply permaculture techniques, which are agricultural ecosystems designed to be sustainable and self-sufficient. Talk to your local authorities to see what is possible. The stronger and more resilient you make your community, the less likely it is that it will crumble around you when something goes wrong.

# 6 HARVESTING THE WILD

Besides growing your own crops, start noticing what you can harvest from the wild. "The wild" can even include the city. Plants like dandelion, cattails and purslane all grow abundantly across the continental US, in both urban and rural areas.

Practice caution. Learn what toxic lookalikes exist in your area, harvest only in non-polluted areas that have low human traffic. Test each plant in small amounts because some people may exhibit allergies to certain plants. If you're interested in learning more, I've written a beginner's guide, "Forging - A Beginner's Guide to Wild Edible and Medicinal Plants" (http://byjillb.com), which covers ten common forageable plants that grow in the US.

Effort and calorie-wise, meat is a far better protein and calorie source than plants. If you already hunt and fish, that is an excellent start. However, when things go wrong and the hordes from the cities try to hunt for food outside the city limits, don't count on being able to hunt for deer. It has happened before - in states like Missouri in the 19th century where unchecked hunting and habitat destruction brought the estimated deer population down to about 400 in the *entire state*.

If history is to be our teacher, the deer population will likely be decimated by a hungry and now much larger human population in a long-term emergency scenario. Instead, start paying attention to the smaller animals in your environment that you can possibly hunt and trap. Animals like birds or water crustaceans like crayfish.

Prepare yourself mentally now, instead of when things are bad. Think about how far you are willing to, or may need to go, to keep yourself and your family alive. Are you willing to possibly even eat insects to survive? There is no right or wrong answer, only the answer than you can live with.

# 7 Cookware

Of course, your food is useless if you do not know how to use or cook it. This is why it's important that your stockpile is continually consumed and replenished. In fact, you should be able to use everything I suggest in this book in your day-to-day frugal life. Do not buy anything that does not meld with your everyday needs. That said, I recommend investing in two pieces of cookware - an antique cast iron skillet, and a good quality Dutch oven.

A Dutch oven is good for making soups, stews, casseroles, roasts and even baking bread; while a cast-iron pan is good for frying, sauteing, pan-frying, searing and even baking. One thing to avoid, however, is cooking acidic foods like tomatoes in cast iron because the iron may impart an off-flavor to the food.

Avoid buying new cast-iron pans because they are usually not sanded and have surfaces that are too rough to cook properly on. Good places to find antique cast-iron pans include flea markets, estate sales, garage sales or thrift stores. If you're lucky, you'll be able to find a pan for about $10. I consider it a must-have in every frugal kitchen - your pan will last a few lifetimes if you take care of it.

## Caring for Your Cast-Iron Pan

Don't turn down an antique cast-iron pan which may be rusted or encrusted in old buildup - it can be saved with a little elbow grease. There are a couple of ways to remove buildup. The first is by spraying oven cleaner over the pan and allowing it to set before washing it off. Repeat the process until all the residue is removed.

The other method, requires more attention but uses only lye instead of oven-cleaning chemicals. **Caution: Lye is highly corrosive. Wear protective gloves and eye goggles and carry out the process outdoors or in a very well-ventilated area, away from other people or animals.** Use 100% or food-grade lye and not drain cleaners which normally contains other additives.

Add 2.5 gallons of water into a clean heavy duty plastic trash can or into a clean plastic food bucket. Carefully add half a pound of lye to the water, stirring it with a wooden spoon or paint stick until all the lye has dissolved. **Always add lye to water, never water to lye, which will cause an explosive reaction.**

Gently put the pan into the lye solution, making sure that it's completely submerged. You will need to soak it for between a few days to several weeks, depending on how thick the buildup is. Wipe the pan's surface with a soft brush or sponge to see if the buildup has dissolved. Do not use metal scrubbers or anything hard and coarse which will scratch the pan's surface. Also remember to avoid direct skin contact with the lye by wearing rubber gloves during this process. Allow the pan to soak in the lye for a few more days if some parts remain encrusted.

When you have sufficiently removed the buildup, wear rubber gloves and scrub the pan with a plastic brush. Rinse the pan in a bath of clean water. Neutralize the pan by soaking it in a solution of one part distilled white vinegar to one part water for 30 minutes. You can remove any remaining patches of buildup buy scrubbing the area with salt for extra abrasion. Soak the pan in the vinegar bath for another 15 minutes before rinsing it with clean water and drying it completely.


## Seasoning the Pan

Cast-iron needs to be seasoned immediately to prevent it from rusting. This basically involves sealing the iron surface using a vegetable oil coating. Avoid using oils with low smoke points, like butter or olive oil. I like using avocado oil which is a an oil with a high smoke point. (Costco is currently the cheapest place that I know of to purchase avocado oil.)

To prepare your pan, heat it on the stovetop or in a 200-degree oven for 10 minutes. Using oven mitts, apply a thin coat of vegetable oil with a new paper towel. Wipe any excess oil away. Preheat the oven to 500 degrees F and place the pan upside in the oven to bake for an hour. Turn the oven off after an hour and allow the pan to cool inside. Repeat the process 3-5 times more before cooking with the pan.

Maintain the seasoned pan by rising the pan with hot water and using a non-abrasive brush. Do not use soap or wash it in a dishwasher. You can, however, use some salt to add extra cleaning abrasion. Dry the pan immediately to prevent it from rusting. If the pan rusts, scrub the rust off and re-season it. Over time, you may need to re-apply oil to the pan to restore the non-stick surface.

## 8 COOKING WITHOUT REGULAR UTILITIES

Your two pieces of cookware should go a long way in a worst-case scenario where your regular stove top no longer runs because utilities have been cut. If you are lucky enough to have a wood stove with a flat surface, learn to cook on it.

With a cast iron pan and a hot wood stove, you can prepare a range of meals - from making something as simple as toast, to preparing meals in your cast-iron pan. I have also produced the most delicious stews in a dutch oven cooked on a smoldering wood stove overnight. I could probably write a whole book on cooking on the wood stove but that would digress from the main topic of this book so I'll discuss a simple and forgiving recipe - the stew.

## Homestead Stew

To make a simple stew, cube vegetables into one-inch pieces. The possibilities are endless but I normally stew root vegetables like carrots, turnips, rutabagas and potatoes together. Vegetables may include squashes, tomatoes (in moderation), corn kernels, onions, kale and celery. Avoid adding broccoli or bell peppers, which impart off-flavors or bitterness to the soup.

You can also add dried beans like chickpeas or navy beans. There is no need to pre-soak beans if they are simmered overnight in the stew. Cubed or shredded meat is optional but adds heartiness to the stews. I'm often too lazy to even cube the meat and end up just cutting it into pieces with a pair of kitchen shears while it's stewing. It's usually best to use one kind of meat in the stew.

Cover your ingredients with water or even better, homemade bone broth. Place the Dutch oven, covered, on your heat source to stew. Add your seasonings - salt and any other herbs like oregano, sage, tarragon and/or thyme. Varying the ingredients and seasonings will naturally yield different cuisine flavors.

Check your stew often if your heat source is running on high heat because the liquid will boil off quickly. Top it with more water to cover the ingredients as needed. If you have enough liquid in it, you can keep the covered Dutch oven overnight on smouldering heat.

If you don't have a wood stove but have some space, consider making a fire pit (if your jurisdiction allows for it) or investing in a charcoal barbecue grill. Let people know that you're looking for a grill and if you're lucky, you might be gifted one. Otherwise, you might be able to find one for free or very cheap on Craigslist or through a Facebook local trading group.

If you're unable to get one used, barbecue grills often go on clearance at most big box stores after the summer season. Many stores like Target will also knock an additional 10% off the price of display models if you ask. Using the Target RedCard will yield an additional 5% off. If you are buying from Lowes or Home Depot, you can also get a Lowes 10% off coupon from the Post Office. Just ask them for the

Mover's Coupon Packet. Home Depot accepts competitor coupons so you should be able to use it there as well.

Practice cooking on your charcoal grill. Try preparing a variety of foods including meats and stews. I recommend investing in a flint striker or a magnesium fire starter, which is available for about $10 at Amazon, and is a more reliable fire starter in a range of conditions. You can use anything from cardboard egg cartons and crumpled non-glossy newspapers to dry pine cones or brown Cattail seed heads for fire starters.

The reason why I prefer a barbecue grill over a propane one is even though propane has a much longer lifespan than most other fuels, you'll need a source. You can, on the other hand, make your own charcoal from untreated wood if the going gets tough.

## Making Charcoal

**Warning: Always make sure that you conduct burns with your local fire department's approval. In drought-prone areas, burns are only allowed at specific times/days.**

There are two ways to make charcoal - the indirect (bottom lit) and the direct (top lit). The direct version requires more attention and finesse. You will basically need a two steel drum or buckets, one that can fit inside the other, and wood.

To make a larger amount of charcoal, you'll need a 55-gallon steel drum with a smaller steel drum that will fit in it. Unfortunately 55-gallon steel drums aren't very easy to find these days but you may be able to buy one from your local garage, metal scrapper or even Craigslist.

Cut a hole at the base of the larger drum to feed the wood though. Drill vent holes on the bottom of a smaller steel drum. Place the smaller drum on a steel grate placed on the bottom of the large drum such that there is still enough room to make a fire in the large drum. Burn off any contaminants in the smaller drum by firing up the set up consisting of the empty smaller drum in the larger one.

Fill the smaller drum with the wood for the charcoal-making and make sure that the lid is secured in. The wood should be untreated with any nails removed. The lid of the larger drum should also secured to retain the heat. Feed more fire through the bottom of the larger drum. After about 45 minutes of burning, gases and flames will start spewing from the drum. After another 5 minutes, the charcoal should be ready.

If you'd like to find out more about the process, Dan Gill best describes the charcoal-making process and the results of his tests on his website at http://www.pine3.info/Charmake.htm.

## Non-Electric Slow Cooker

When you have limited cooking fuels, a way to conserve on them is to invest in a non-electric slow cooker or hay box. In a nutshell, food is heated to boiling point and covered. It is then allowed to boil for 5-15 minutes before it is placed in the insulated hay box to continue cooking.

Originally invented around the early 19th century as a way to conserve cooking fuel, the hay box still comes in handy if cooking fuels are in short supply. Traditional versions are made by filling a wooden box with insulating material such as straw or hay and setting the pot in the middle before covering the top with more insulation.

Modern variations include wrapping your boiling pot in a cotton towel then wrapping a sleeping bag around it, to using a Wonder Oven, which is reminiscent of a bean bag with a hole in the middle for your pot. If you're good at sewing, you can make your own. Iwillprepare.com has generously provided a free sewing pattern which you can download at http://hyperurl.co/sewwonderoven. Otherwise, you can buy them for about $60 on Amazon or Etsy. Wonder Ovens will also work as insulators to help to keep things cold. Bear in mind that they are bulky but can double as a pillow.

If you're concerned about the food temperature falling into the danger zone while your food is stewing in the hay box, bring it back up to a boil for 10 minutes on the stove before consumption.

## Solar Cooker

Solar cookers are another great way to heat, cook, bake or even pasteurize food and drinks with a free renewal energy source - solar power. Of course, the downside of using a solar cooker is that its use is limited by sun exposure. Winter is generally not a good time to use a solar cooker.

The concept is simple and involves placing your pot in a reflective box or container. Dark colored cookware absorbs heat better and therefore works better than reflective or light-colored cookware. Commercial versions retail for about $300 but you can make your own for a fraction of the price. You can find a myriad of solar cooker plans from http://solarcooking.org/plans/.

## A Very Simple Rocket-like Stove

If you have limited space, you can still make make a very simple rocket-like stove using a metal coffee can that does not have an inner plastic lining. Remove any outer labels before turning your coffee can into a rocket stove.

On the bottom of the can, cut a rectangular hole, large enough to feed kindling in. Do not cut any part of the base away. The following step is optional but improves the stove. Form a cylinder with a piece of hardware cloth or wire mesh. The wire cylinder should be  a little shorter than the can's height and be about the 1/2 - 2/3 the diameter of the can. Slowly flatten the opposite sides of the cylinder and bend it to form a hollow U-shape. Insert the wire into the coffee can such that the bottom of the "U" directly faces the opening that you cut out. Place a grate or hardware cloth on top of the coffee can.

Feed your kindling through the cutout hole at the bottom of the coffee can. You can cook on your rocket stove once you have a consistent fire going in it. **Be careful: The rocket stove will be hot and will stay hot for quite a while after the fire dies out.** An advantage of using a rocket stove is that it allows you to cook using things can you can forage for such as twigs. Do not burn treated wood. Wood pallets are a good wood source if you live in the city.

## 9 COMPOSTING TOILETS

What goes in, must of course, come out. In cases where water is scarce, or where utilities are limited, using a composting toilet may be a good option. Note though, that using composting toilets may be against local regulations and would only be an option in emergency situations. There are commercially available composting toilets with all kinds of bells and whistles, but your composting toilet can be as basic as using a 5-gallon plastic bucket with appropriate fine organic material to cover your waste.

In "Mrs Owen's Beginning Prepper Guide For Women: Looking To The Future With Joy", Katie Owens suggests buying swimming noodles on seasonal clearance. Each one can be slit to its middle, lengthwise and used as a toilet seat by wrapping it around the bucket rim.

Since we currently live in an RV without a septic tank on our homestead full-time while we save money to build a house, I opted to purchase a camping "tote-able" toilet seat and lid for about $15 online instead. A camping toilet seat is very much like a regular toilet seat and snaps onto most plastic buckets.

To keep the buckets from accumulating too much liquid, urinate and defecate in different buckets. Urine is much easier to dispose of so try to avoid adding more "muck" into your solid waste toilet. Dispose of the urine daily to prevent smells from developing. The urine can be disposed off in a compost pile, under mature trees, shrubs and on lawns but need to be diluted in a ratio of 1 part urine to at least 3 parts water before applying it on maturing or potted plants.

To prepare your solid waste bucket, place about 2-3 inches of covering material at the bottom of the bucket before use. Cover any solid waste completely with the covering material. We've found good success using peat moss as a covering. Others report success using coconut coir. However, depending on where you live, these may not necessarily easy to find in tough times.

Other covering options include sawdust from untreated wood, ground corn cobs, dried leaf crumbles or leaf mold. Do not use cedar, which will not compost properly. Also avoid using hay, straw or grass clippings, which don't absorb liquid. They will, however, work to cover the final humanure compost pile.

For our family of four (two adults and two young children), a 5-gallon bucket fills up in about 7-10 days. The bucket is then placed in a shed, uncovered and away from human or animal traffic. It is allowed to sit undisturbed for another 4 weeks while we rotate to our next 5-gallon bucket (we use a total of five buckets in rotation). If properly taken care of, the toilet and its contents should not smell bad.

After the fourth week, the bucket is emptied into a 32-gallon trash can. The process of transferring the waste-compost is not the most pleasant experience. To reduce the problem of any liquid collected in the bucket, we sprinkle more peat-covering on top of the waste; cover it with a lid, then carefully tip and bang the bucket, allowing the peat to coat the bucket sides. This helps to loosen the waste-mass and to absorb the liquid in the bucket. Dump the contents into the trashcan and add more covering over the new waste.

Once filled, we start filling the next large container and allow the waste to compost for a year before using it for ornamental planting beds or as a side dressing for trees. We currently live in Southern Oregon which has mild winters. If you live in a climate with cold and/or long winters, you might need to give your humanure more time to compost.

The compost should not smell. Different putrid smells indicate different composting problems. Fruity or alcoholic smells suggest too much starch or simple sugars; ammonia suggests too little carbon and hydrogen sulfide (rotten egg smell) is a sign of the pile lacking air. Saw dust, coarsely ground charcoal or sandy soil will respectively help to fix these problems. However, sandy soil will not compost and should be added sparingly. If maggots appear, cover the pile with more covering material. This additional layer will starve the maggots of access to any exposed waste matter.

If you're out of toilet paper, non-glossy newspaper or phonebook paper crumpled over a few times will work. Unless you know what you're doing, avoid using leaves, some of which can cause skin irritation. Dealing with humanure is often met with trepidation. However, as long as you practice standard personal hygiene, using and maintaining a composting toilet should not pose problems. Wash your hands well with soap and clean water after using and tending to the toilet.

# 10 PERSONAL HYGIENE

## Bathing

If you are blessed with a lot of sun, consider using a solar shower (about $10 from Amazon or Walmart), which is basically a hose attached to a black 5-gallon bag that absorbs solar heat. For most people, solar showers are not an option in winter. Instead, we use two stock pots - one to boil water in, and the other with some cold water. The boiling water is added to the cold water until we achieve the desired temperature. Both options are water-conservative.

## Dental Hygiene

If you need to conserve water even more, use a spray bottle for lesser water uses like dampening your toothbrush. Keeping your dental hygiene up is important in keeping your overall health up. For emergency scenarios, you can brush your teeth using a 1:1 mix of baking soda and salt. Stocking up on floss is optional but recommended.

## Soap

I am a big fan of making and using my own lye soap. We've not only saved so much money by using homemade soap for all our washing needs, we've also reduced packaging waste and cured ourselves of red, dry skin and itchy scalp problems.

In "The Modern American Frugal Housewife Book #3 - Moms Edition", I detailed the ways in which you can make soap frugally, including using rancid oils if needed. Otherwise, you can use any animal or nut fat or vegetable oil as your soap base. Different oils will give the soap different properties.

In addition to your oil, you'll also need lye to saponify the oils into soap. You can use drain cleaner **only if** it is 100% lye. Roebic Laboratories Heavy Duty Drain Cleaner is one of the few drain cleaners that is 100% lye and is available at Lowes (about $15 for 2 lbs). This is not the cheapest way to buy lye but is a decent way to buy a small amount of lye locally (assuming that you have a Lowes nearby). If you are looking to make soap in bulk, you can buy it by the case from Essential Depot (http://bit.ly/1v7V3rE)* for a fraction of the price that Lowe's charges.

In the past, being able to produce hard soap was an art form, and a source of pride for housewives. Back then, lye water was boiled in a large stainless steel or cast iron pot before the lard was slowly added. The mixture was continually stirred and more lye was added until it attained a syrup thickness. Soap could also be made hard by the addition of salt.

The soap would then poured into container molds to cool and cure before being cut into bars. The final properties of the soap including hardness and sudsing depends on the lye water concentration, the type of ashes used, and the type of fat used. Regardless, even a "failed" soft or liquid soap can be used for washing, shampooing and laundering, just as we use liquid soap today.

## Soap Making Process

You will need:

- a kitchen scale to weigh everything (I put it in a ziploc bag to protect it from spills)
- 100% lye
- Your fat(s)
- 2 stainless steel or plastic containers to mix the lye in and for the saponification process
- An immersion blender to mix everything (optional but recommended)
- Thermometer
- A mold for your soap - I just used a shoe box lined with a plastic bag
- Gloves and safety goggles

### Method

1. Use soapcalc (http://bit.ly/1AB4KB6) to calculate your ingredients.
2. Pour the water into one of your containers.
3. Put on your gloves and safety goggles.
4. In a well-ventilated area or outdoors, add lye to the water. **ALWAYS add lye to water.** Adding water to lye will cause an explosive reaction.
5. Stir the mixture with a plastic spoon. Allow the lye solution to cool.
6. In another stainless steel container, melt all the oils over medium-low heat.
7. Allow the oils to cool to about 96°F.

8. Add the lye to the oil and stir constantly.
9. When a trace forms (ie, when you can trace a line in the mixture), you may add essential oils. Blend some more.
10. Pour the mixture into your mold and allow it to cure for a week before cutting.

# Homemade Lye

It's better to use commercial lye for soap-making because it provides consistency to your soap recipes. However, in the event that commercial lye isn't available, you can make your own using wood ash. Our ancestors got by without commercial lye. In fact, Lydia Maria Child, the author of the inspiration of this series, "The American Frugal Housewife" (1833), also discussed the lye-making process in her book.

Lye should only be made from wood ash and not other kinds of ash like charcoal. It's best to use hardwood ash like Oak or Maple, and not ash from softwoods like Pine, which is too resinous. Homemade lye technically produces potassium hydroxide, which is the basis of liquid soap, rather that sodium hydroxide which we use to make hard soap.

Wood ash lye is traditionally made in a wooden barrel which, these days are not easy to come by. Do not use metal, which the lye will corrode. You can, however, use a plastic 5-gallon bucket instead. Drill a neat small hole, about 1/8th of an inch in diameter, about an inch above the bottom on one side of the bucket. This hole must be the size of a cork or stopper to stop the hole up as needed.

Ensure that your wood ash is cold before scooping it into the stopped-up bucket. Only use the fine ash, not the wood chunks and compact it into the bucket. Elevate the bucket high enough on a sturdy support such that you can place a stainless steel pot under the drilled bucket hole.

Boil enough water, preferably rainwater, which is softer, to fill half the capacity of the bucket. Carefully pour the hot water over the ashes. Expect the water to bubble and hiss when it touches the ashes. Give the water time to seep down, undisturbed, before adding any remaining water. Place the receiving stock pot under the drilled hole before removing the stopper and allow the caustic lye water to drip out and collect in the pot. This process may take as long as a few days.

Once you've collected the lye, wear gloves and safety goggles and warm the lye water before re-pouring it over the stopped up bucket of ashes. Do not add boiling lye water which may melt your bucket. Reposition the pot under the drilled hole and unstopper it. Allow the lye water to drip out again. This process helps to concentrate the lye water.

Naturally, your lye water will vary in concentration. Old World techniques include using eggs, potatoes or chicken feathers to test the lye water. If an egg or potato floats just below halfway in the lye, or if a feather starts to dissolve in the lye water, it is the right strength. If the egg does not float or the feather does not start to dissolve, the lye water needs to be boiled down. Conversely, if the egg jumps out of the lye too fast, or if the feather dissolves very quickly, the lye is too strong and needs to be gradually diluted by the cup with rainwater.

Besides using lye water to make soap, it can also be used to sanitize toilets or non-carpeted floors. Any lye water application should be followed with a clean, cold water rinse. Test on a small area because applying your lye water to large areas. Although food preservation deserves at least a book on its own if not more, I will also mention that lye can also used to preserve food. However, alkaline preservation techniques are not as common as acidic preservation.

Although lye is not poisonous per se, it is highly corrosive. Always exercise care when using or handling lye. Always wear rubber gloves when using it. Keep children and animals away from it and always use cold water to rinse it off. Hot water makes lye more active. Lye is basic and can always be neutralized by acids like vinegars and citric acids (found in lemon juice etc).

## Diapers and Sanitary Pads

Most survival books written by men don't seem to acknowledge this but women have additional personal care needs. Stocking up on disposal pads and diapers is not a sustainable solution because they cannot be reused and contribute to your non-compostable waste pile. Keeping your waste pile to a minimum is important in keeping vermin and disease at bay.

You can buy cloth pads and diapers online from sites like Etsy but you can also sew them yourself. For pads, good fabric options include high quality polar fleece or felted wool for the waterproof layer; Terry cloth or cotton batting for the absorbent layer; and good quality flannel for the top layer.

In "The Modern American Frugal Housewife Book #3 - Moms Edition", I discussed the issue of diaper options more at length. In an long-term emergency prepper situation, reusable diapers, like cloth menstrual pads, are without a doubt the best way to go. Cotton, bamboo fiber, wool and polyester fleece are all possible options for cloth diapers. You can find a list of links to many free diaper patterns online or at zany-zebra.com (http://hyperurl.co/diaperpatterns). Naturally, dark patterned fabrics will help to hide stains better than light solid colors.

You can use fabrics that you have on hand or purchase it new. Either way, wash everything before sewing because the fabrics will shrink after washing. Tipnut.com (http://hyperurl.co/padstyles) lists the different pad styles that are available.

Ecofriendlyfamily.com (http://hyperurl.co/freepadpattern) also has free patterns available online.

To be honest, I'm not a fan of sewing. I'm reasonably apt at it but would rather be doing something else. You can make no-sew diapers by folding them. Believe it or not, cloth diapers can be folded from flat sheets. 1st-time-mothers.com (http://hyperurl.co/folddiaper) provides a good illustration on how to fold diapers from a flat cloth sheet.

Similarly, you can make decent no-sew menstrual pads by using washed, absorbent terry cloth dish towels or cut up old wool sweaters. Fold them into rectangles three-layers thick, that are about 3-4 inches by 10-12 inches. Snug underwear will secure the pad in place. You may need to use two wash cloths for heavier flows. Naturally, this option is bulkier than sewn pads.

If you don't want to bother with pads at all, try using a reusable menstrual cup. I've not tried these myself but there are many brands including Diva, Lena and Blossom, all of which are available online or at most retail stores. The downside of these cups is that you might not be able to replace them easily in dire situations.

## Washing

Of course, you will need to wash your reusable pads and cloth diapers to maintain them. Although you can machine wash cloth pads and diapers, I will assume that machine washing is limited when times are tough. Washing the pads is pretty easy. For sanitary reasons, I prefer to wash them as soon as possible rather than keeping them in a cloth sack before washing them all at once. Washing the pads as you go also means that you have more clean pads on hand.

To wash, run cold water over the pads to remove as much blood as possible. If you need to conserve water, you can soak the pad(s) in a bucket of cold water instead. Never use warm or hot water, which will set the blood into the fabric, thereby staining it. Place the rinsed-off pads in a bucket of cold water with some soap added.

If you have more than menstrual pads to hand-wash, you can purchase mobile hand washers from Amazon or BePrepared.com for about $15. You can also make your own hand washer by drilling a few holes into a new plunger. Using a mobile washer is surprisingly simple process. It is similar to plunging your clothing in a bucket of soapy water, all without any need for electricity or an expensive washer. Plunge the laundry or pad(s) for about 10 minutes or until clean.

Rinse the laundry well, squeeze it dry then air dry them on a clothesline. If you have a lot of laundry or heavy clothing to squeeze dry, make holes on the bottom of a 5-gallon plastic bucket. Collect all your wet laundry in the drilled bucket then place the washing bucket, still filled with the water, on top of the wet laundry. The weight of the top bucket will help to squeeze the excess water out of the laundry.

Cloth diapers can be washed in a bucket in a fashion similar to washing cloth pads. Dispose of any solid waste into your toilet. The main difference with washing cloth diapers versus cloth pads is the use of hot water instead of cold. Use soapy water at as high a temperature as possible before plunging the diapers clean. You may need to use more than one soapy water change. Once clean, do a final rinse with clean water before squeezing it dry and air drying it on a clothesline.

# 11 CLOTHING

Like food, your prepper clothing should be part of your everyday clothe use. It should generally not be anything specially marked as "prepper clothing". That said, I like clothes that are not necessarily cheap, but are frugal. That is, that they are durable and of good quality.

Other qualities in "prepper" clothing to consider include being able to withstand a lot of wear, being easy to wash and dry by hand, and if the clothes can be mended easily. These properties will help you to get by when times are tough. If they serve more than one purpose (for example a raincoat and a light jacket), all the better.

In terms of material, cotton is excellent for breathability and lightness in warm or tropical climates but takes a long time to dry. 100% cotton also tends to wear out more quickly. In non-tropical climates a 50% cotton, 50% synthetic material might be a better choice.

In colder climates, I suggest having a mix of layered clothing. For Colorado winters for example, I had two pairs of synthetic thermal underwear to serve as the base clothing layer. I rarely used them since my husband is the one who does most of the outside winter work. He on the other hand, has quite a few sets for everyday outdoor winter use.

For bottoms, jeans and cargo pants are good choices for climates that are less cold. I like cargo pants because of the extra pockets. For colder weather, I like fleece. It's affordable, comfortable, warm and water resistant. It also dries quickly and is easy to sew with because it doesn't fray. Add additional clothing layers according to your environment.

I generally prefer loose-fitting T-shirts for comfort. Looser clothing also allow you to wear under layers and to conceal items or weapons, if needed. Avoid colors that attract attention. Wear camo clothing with caution. Landscape-appropriate camo is great if it serves as a camouflage when you need to hunt or hide in the open. It's not so great if that camo is inappropriate, for example, wearing jungle camo in a snow-white landscape.

It's also not a good idea to call attention to yourself because that attention can very easily be negative. If you are in the city or suburbs, wearing camo (or other colors like navy blue which may be construed as an authority figure uniform,) may also make you stand out - not necessarily a good thing.

Consider wearing solid dull colors like grey or black, since they are less likely to draw attention and hide stains better. These stains can be as benign as stains from gardening or from working around the home. Tan is also a decent color option because it develops stains from your surroundings, effectively making a "custom" camo.

In Colorado, my husband normally needed heavy duty winter gloves, two layers of socks in snow boots and four to five layers of clothing for winter outdoor duties. These layers included a thermal under layer, a t-shirt, a fleece sweater or pullover, a winter vest and a waterproof puffy down jacket to go over everything. (You get the picture.)

Now that we live in Southern Oregon, we are slowly learning what new clothes we need to deal with the milder but much wetter climate. There is no "right" kind of clothing, only what is right for your environment and situation. What is important is to figure out what you need now, instead of needing it but not having it when a situation gets bad.

## Footwear

Like clothing, buy footwear that you can use now. Invest in socks that fit your feet rather than buying one-size-fits-most socks which do not normally fit as well. Like ill-fitting shoes, ill-fitting socks can be a cause of discomfort and foot blisters. Prepper outdoor shoes should be able to withstand a lot of walking or outdoor activities such as gardening or digging. Shop for shoes in the afternoon, when your feet are most expanded; and choose the size that fits your bigger foot. The shoe should support the ankles and arches well.

Choose footwear materials to suit your climate and environment. For example, full-grain leather shoes are good for wet conditions. In hotter climates, shoes that provide air flow like Crocs or Tevas are more practical. The downside to more foot ventilation is that your feet are not as well protected. These shoes also tend to be less durable than sturdier-built shoes. Figure out what works best for *you*. Break your shoes in by walking around in them for increasing periods of time, first by walking around the house then gradually walking longer and longer distances outside.

Make sure that your boots are properly laced and that the laces are of good quality. If your shoes come with inferior laces, upgrade them to paracord or Fire Laces which are made from 550-pound paracord with lace tips that are integrated with Ferro rods for fire-starting. Fire Laces are reasonably affordable, costing about $15-$20 on Amazon.

Of course, the frugal housewife takes care of her possessions. Follow the manufacturer's care instructions for your shoes. Waterproofing outdoor boots will normally help to extend their life. After each use, remove the dirt and grime from the threads in the soles. Remove the inserts from the shoes to allow both the shoes and the inserts to air dry. Like most other things, store your footwear out of direct sunlight, cold temperatures and other environmental extremes.

## Children's Clothing

Naturally, children have very similar clothing needs with one obvious difference - their increasing size. I like to prep for my kids' clothing needs by keeping an eye out for clothes two sizes up. That way, we always have clothing available when we need it. In "The Modern American Frugal Housewife Book #3 - Moms Edition" (http://byjillb.com), I discussed in detail ways to procure kid's clothing for free or at very low cost.

In a nutshell, always let it be known amongst everyone you know that you're on a lookout for hand-me-downs. Depending on where you live, Craigslist.org or local Facebook garage sale or mommy groups might also be a good place to find hand-me-downs. Otherwise, Target and Kohls are good places to find kid's clothing at very low sale or clearance prices. Details on how to stack deals to the maximum are laid out in Book #3. I avoid buying at consignment stores because I've found that they rarely offer prices that can beat big-box store sales (after deal stacking).

Keep a good sewing kit on hand - threads, needles, scissors, sewing pins, a pin cushion, sewing chalk and a measuring tape. Learn the basics of sewing and mending. Online videos are your friends if you want to learn for free.

If you want to extreme prep, consider investing in a foot-pedal or Treadle powered sewing machine, like our foremothers used. It is, however, not cheap at around $300. I don't recommend it unless you like to sew. With a sewing machine and supplies, you can pretty much sew whatever you need from fabric on hand. Many women, especially rural ones, did so before the mid-twentieth century.

If you develop a knack for sewing, consider turning it into a business for an additional income stream. Depending on what you make, Handmade by Amazon or Etsy.com would probably be the better platforms to launch your business from. I will discuss developing multiple income streams as part of your prepper arsenal in a later chapter.

## 12 HEALTH

## Prescriptions

Before we go further, I need to discuss a very important topic - health. Keeping yourself fit in body and sound of mind is very important, particularly when times are difficult. Like all the topics covered in the previous chapters, start working on yourself now. Keep fit and exercise. If you have bad habits like smoking, try to quit. Addictive habits may be more difficult to break or continue in hard times.

Unfortunately, not everyone starts off in the peak of health. There isn't a lot in terms of prep when it comes to prescription drugs unless you're able to convince your doctor to prescribe extra medication for you. It may be as simple as asking your doctor if you can get more medication in case of an emergency. Of course, your success rate will vary.

Practice mindfulness. Believe me, I know that it's not always easy to do, especially if you live in an RV and have two young kids bickering while you're trying. to. get. this. book. done. I've found that keeping note of small things in my life that I'm grateful for helps my overall mental well-being. If you need a little guidance, try Happify (http://happify.com), which has both free and paid services.

## Antibiotics

There are eight different kinds of fish antibiotics - Fish-Cillin, Fish-Cin, Fish-Flox, Fish-Penn, Fish-Mox, Fish-Sulfa and Fish-Zol. Each has its own effects, side-effects and interactions with other medications or supplements. There is a lot of discussion among prepper circles regarding stockpiling fish antibiotics. The reason is that you can buy copious amounts of these antibiotics without a prescription. Note that while they may be the same kinds of antibiotics as the human version, there may also be additives or fish supplements that you want to avoid. Websites like Drugs.com offer more information on antibiotics.

Make sure that you study each one carefully before you decide on which one you may want to use. Antibiotics have expiration dates, after which they are less effective. They should always be used with caution. They can only be used for bacterial infections and not viral ones. Excessive use will render them ineffective. I am not a medical professional. Stockpile and use at your own discretion and risk.

## First-Aid

Of course, it is always prudent to be prepared. Take a first aid or CPR course. You may be able to find a class through The Red Cross, a local community college, the YMCA or a local recreational center. "Advanced First Aid Afloat" (Cornell Maritime Pr, 2009) by Dr. Peter F. Eastman, MD., is a good book for further reading.

Keep a small stock of basic first-aid supplies and equipment like gauzes, bandages, tweezers and splints; antibiotic creams and some painkillers. You can buy these items inexpensively from local stores or online.

## Herbal Remedies

Being familiar with herbal remedies is very helpful especially when medical help isn't readily available. Many herbal and traditional home remedies are surprisingly effective. For example, fresh peeled garlic cloves left to infuse in unadulterated (preferably raw and organic) honey for as long as possible has been surprisingly effective in keeping colds at bay for my family. As an extra bonus, garlic preserved in honey this way lasts indefinitely without refrigeration.

To make honey-fermented garlic, place peeled garlic cloves in a glass jar, leaving 1-2 inches of head-space. Cover the cloves in honey. Expect the cloves to float to the top. Cover the jar loosely to allow any air produced from the fermentation process to escape. The honey may ferment and bubble lightly or vigorously. The bubbling or lack thereof is a normal process.

Push the garlic cloves with a clean, dry utensil back under the honey every day. Otherwise, the cloves that are not submerged under the honey for an extended period of time will mold. The honey will become less viscous over time and the garlic will darken. It may even turn blue or greenish in color. All are normal processes.

If you want to take your prepping to another level, consider growing a medicinal garden. Medicinal gardening is a huge topic but in "Medicinal Herb Gardening - 10 Plants for The Self-Reliant Homestead Prepper" (http://byjillb.com), I narrowed down a list of medicinal plants that the homesteader/prepper may wish to include in their self-reliance plan. These plants were carefully chosen for their relative cultivation ease, ease of cultivation in most of the Continental US, medicinal prowess, for having uses beyond the medicinal.

Even if you have limited growing space, all is not lost. You can still grow cayenne pepper. Although it is a tropical plant, it can easily be grown in containers even in the smallest of apartments. Almost everyone knows that the pepper pods are edible but did you know that pepper leaves are edible when cooked? It is delicious.

Amongst many herbal uses, cayenne pepper can be used to prevent shock (when consumed). Cayenne pepper powder can also be used externally to stop profuse bleeding. Believe it or not, when applied in this manner, it doesn't sting the skin. If you're unable to keep fresh cayenne on hand, a bottle of dried cayenne powder, usually available for less than $5 from any grocery store, will do the job.

## 13 FINANCIAL SECURITY

Now that we have covered our basic needs of water, food, clothing and health, we can take things a little further by making ourselves more financially resilient. There are many books that discuss financial security in depth. In a nutshell, reducing debt and increasing your income and savings are the main factors in contributing to your financial security. In fact, I have discussed a multitude of ideas on how to stretch your money throughout this Modern American Frugal Housewife series.

## Increasing Income Streams

Yes, having a steady job that pays well can contribute to financial security. Unfortunately, the days of having a steady job with one company your whole life and generous pensions are gone. Having one job is one income stream.

All your eggs are in one (job) basket - a risky position to be in. You're placed in a perilous position if the company folds, you get laid off or if your hours are cut. We homesteaders do not like putting all our eggs in one basket, either figuratively or literally. I sadly learned this painful lesson one day when I accidentally dropped my one basket full of eggs and kissed the eggs for that day goodbye.

Never again. To lower your financial security risk, look into developing multiple income streams. It's not as complicated as it sounds. More income streams may involve a second job with another company or running your own business or both!

Think about what you can do or are good at. The possibilities are endless - babysitting, becoming a driver through Uber.com or Lyft.com, renting out unused space on Airbnb.com, running errands or performing services through Craigslist or TaskRabbit.com, tutoring, consulting, freelancing and more.

We are so lucky to live in a time where you can easily start and run a business. Depending on your interest, you can turn a lot of prepping ideas covered in this book into a business. Do you like canning or dehydrating food? Try selling dry mixes or canned jams or jellies according to your state's regulations. Like to garden? You can try selling seeds, root-stocks, seedlings, plants, produce and/or flowers. Some of these items can be turned into additional products like herbal salves, for example. Like to sew or work with your hands? You can sell a range of things from clothing to toys to supplies.

I'm a big fan of working from home. It's a huge time, money and gas-saver. Even though I'd held some outside-the-home part-time jobs, a bulk of my working life has involved working from home - running businesses on eBay, Etsy and Amazon; inventing and selling our Chicken Armor poultry saddles (http://chickenarmor.com), offering online tutoring and customer service and currently, writing books.

I like publishing books because of its passive income potential. If you're interested in learning more about how to start your own online or indie publishing business, please refer to my Home Business Books (http://byjillb.com), which will guide you through the process of starting up your own small business with little to no upfront cost.

Other passive income possibilities that may work for you include monetizing your YouTube videos, blogs, podcasts; producing apps, T-shirt designs or music; or producing courses and selling them either on your own site or through companies like Udemy.com or Craftsy.com.

Just remember that there are no get-rich-quick schemes here. It takes work and time to build your business and brand. Not everything is going to work or be a good fit for you. I've tried many businesses in my lifetime.

Some, like making custom business signs, were simply not a good fit. It became a drudgery. I hated it. I tried blogging for almost a year and stressed over trying to post content regularly. I wasn't able to gain an audience and I felt like I was spinning my wheels in mud. My blog now lies dead in the depths of the web.

My point is, when it comes to income diversification, you need to try different things. There is no shame in quitting something that doesn't work out for you. If it doesn't, don't keep hitting your head against the wall. Life is too short to force yourself to do something that isn't working out. Try something else that may work for you!

# Reducing Debt

Besides increasing your income, reducing your debt will help your bottom line. Many financial experts' mantra is eliminate "bad debt" like credit cards. "Good debts" like a mortgage and student loans are acceptable. Unfortunately, this is very simplistic. We learned the hard way that all debts affect our emotional well-being.

You might have to think outside the box. What if you have college-aged kids that you need to fund? Consider sending them abroad. Countries like Norway, Iceland and Germany (http://www.studying-in-germany.org) still currently offer a free or very low-cost university education, even to foreign students. Many courses are taught in English.

For us, reducing our debt meant getting rid of a hefty "good debt" - our home loan. Even though we were making a decent income from our businesses, we were shackled by the home payments. It was a long time before we realized that the home we'd thought of as our "forever home" was no longer working for us.

We had changed. We wanted more. We had turned from city-folk to homesteaders and preppers. Living in that home was the catalyst that changed us but it took us a long time to realize that we had outgrown our home and location. It made no sense to break our backs trying to service that "good debt" so we sold the house and moved across the country to a more affordable location and a piece of property that is more suitable for our permaculture plans.

Our journey will probably be the basis of another book but long story short, our mental well-being improved dramatically after we'd decided to make the change. Sometimes it's not about making more - it's about being able to work with a lot less.

Of course, financial security for us as preppers goes a little beyond increasing income, saving money and reducing debt. For us, it also means investing in things that make us more self-reliant. These include building an energy-efficient home, investing in food crops as well as wind and/or solar power, a good wood stove, and good hunting, gardening and building tools.

## Gold & Silver

Gold and silver have long held some intrinsic value. Many use these precious metals as a hedge against the US Dollar, which is now a fiat currency - that is a currency that derives its value from government regulation or law and is not actually backed by a good (usually gold or silver) with intrinsic value.

Governments throughout history have overproduced fiat currencies, causing a currency oversupply which depreciated it. The result is inflation. When the issuing government is no longer willing or able to back a fiat currency, hyperinflation ensues. Examples include post-WWI Austria, Germany and Hungary; Japanese-issued occupation currency before the end of WWII, China after WWII, Yugoslavia in the early 1990s and most recently, Zimbabwe in 2008. Current US deficits and the Fed's seemingly endless quantitative easing puts the US economy and US Dollar at risk.

If you have money, gold is a good prepper choice, especially if you need to bug out. The spot price of gold or silver is the current market price for the metal itself. At the Dec 2015 gold spot price of about $1085 per ounce, gold is a much more compact method of moving away with your wealth. Unlike bags of silver, 1/10th - 1 ounce gold coins can be sewn into clothing or even swallowed to avoid detection. As long as it is recognized as such, gold is accepted just about anywhere. Opt for recognizable gold coins like the Krugerrand, American Gold Eagle, Canadian Gold Maple Leaf, Austrian Gold Philharmonic or the Chinese Gold Panda.

However, you can diversify your precious metal holdings by buying some silver as well. At the time of writing (Dec 2015), the silver spot price is very affordable at about $14.50 per ounce. Many preppers like to buy junk silver or pre-1964 silver coins. These coins effectively gives you a recognizable currency that is divisible in an economic meltdown - very handy for everyday purchases.

Remember that this is not an investment or financial strategy book but a prepper book. When it comes to just about any situation, I believe that diversifying within reason is good. However, I'd caution against investing in more unusual metals like platinum for prepping because these metals are not as easily recognizable and may not be as easy to liquidate as gold or silver.

A prepper's precious metal stash is not an investment but an insurance. After all, you cannot directly consume these metals and can only use them to buy things that you need *if* these things are available for purchase. It's better add both gold and silver to your prepper stash *after* you've invested in tangible goods.

## Cash

Cash is King for disasters that are not related to an economic collapse. Whether a grid-down situation is caused by terrorists, Mother Nature or human error, do not count on ATM machines running or banks being open. Keep enough cash (in different denominations) on hand for your daily necessities. Keep more on hand if you think that you may need to bug-out.

# 14 PERSONAL SAFETY

Financial security aside, we'll now focus on personal safety. History has shown time and again how quickly society can crumble when the infrastructure glitches. Try to avoid drawing attention to yourself (with appropriate clothing choice etc), and to your home by making it look modest with having visible deterrents and not exposing valuables.

Valuables can include items of monetary value as well as water, medical and food supplies. Do not disclose your preps to anyone and certainly not on national TV. Learn to become more aware of your surroundings and be ready to react.

In his book, "The Gift of Fear", security expert Gavin de Becker stated "Americans worship logic, even when it's wrong, and deny intuition, even when it's right". He outlined violence pre-incident indicators that we should always be aware of. Most importantly, always trust your intuition or "gut-feeling" - hesitation, suspicion, doubt, fear, hunches, nagging feelings and dark humor (eg comments that a package may contain a bomb) are all indicators of your defenses at work. Put safety over being embarrassed or hurting a stranger's feelings. Learn self-defense.

For other possible emergencies, keep drinking water, a compass, maps and emergency blankets in your car. In an easily accessible location of your car (not in the glove compartment), keep a glass breaker like an automatic center punch, and a seat-belt cutter on hand. Have extras within reach of other passengers in case you are incapacitated in an accident. Carry a whistle to call for help and a weather-resistant LED flashlight on your keyring. Learn to swim. Community colleges or groups often offer classes at low cost.

If you live in a more populated area, you may want to remove shrubs and bushes where people may hide in and replace glass windows with break-resistant Plexiglas. If you live in a tough area or want to increase your security, install steel bars on windows, replace wooden doors with window-less steel doors with deadbolts. Heavy blackout curtains similar to what Londoners used in WWII during the Blitz, will keep lights showing from the outside.

## Firearms

Many American survivalists encourage having a cache of firearms for when SHTF. Some survivalists even recommend having a gun, even if it's illegal in your area, "just in case". Their theory is that when SHTF, you can join shootouts with the "good guys" against the "bad guys". Easy there, Rambo. I'm going to be a contrarian here. Always abide by your local laws.

Some states are more gun-friendly than others. In most states, you will need to have a concealed gun permit to carry a concealed firearm. Possessing or carrying guns into some areas is illegal. Make sure that you stay on the correct side of the law before investing in firearms. Don't get me wrong, I'm not against having guns - we own a few ourselves, both for personal defense and for hunting. If you're unsure about local gun laws, your local sheriff's department should be able to provide you with necessary information regarding gun possession and ownership.

If it is legal for you to own guns and you'd would like to invest in firearms, a magazine-fed weapon is a good choice for home defense. According to a 2008 RAND Corporation study (http://hyperurl.co/nypdaim) which evaluated the NYPD's firearm training from 1998-2006, the average hit rate during gunfights was just 18%. Without return fire, the NYPD's hit rate was 30%. *30% for real cops.* Anything less than a magazine-fed gun does not give you good odds, especially if you have more than one intruder.

If you live in a state that limits the legal magazine capacity, some companies make clips that allow you to attach two magazines together, which allows you to quickly remove the depleted magazine and to replace it with the fresh one.

For hunting, modern sporting rifles like the AR15 are popular. We also hunt with bow-and-arrow because of the longer hunting season. There are pros and cons of each weapon. Research and choose what is suitable for *you*.

Once you've decided on your weapon, stock up on ammunition. There's already been a long shortage of .22-calibre shells. No one's been really able to give us a reason for this shortage but we buy when we can. You gun is virtually useless without ammo. You need it for practice. You need it to make extra shots. You may need it to make distress shots (learn the universal three-shot distress signal). Do you live in grizzly or moose territory? You need more ammo.

Keep your gun accessible to you but out of reach of children. Teach your children gun safety. If you are bringing kids to someone's home, always make sure that your host keeps their guns out of reach of children. Finally, make sure that you know how to use your gun properly. Like all our other preps, from seeds to flour for cooking, not knowing how to use your gun renders it useless.

## Knives

To be honest, I'm not a big fan of guns. They have their place on the homestead but they're not a regular-use tool. If you've read my books, you'll find that I am a fan of things that have multiple uses.

Knives can be a very useful utility and defense tool. Like choosing a the right kitchen knife which I discussed in "The Modern American Frugal Housewife Book #1 - Home Economics" (http://byjillb.com), you'll need to figure out a knife that works for you.

It should be made well and fit your hands without being too heavy. Keep it sharp by learning how to use a sharpening stone. Our knives are mainly used for processing meat or wood. However, they can also double as self-defense tools. Remember that knives are weapons so make sure you comply with your local knife laws as well!

## 15 WORKING ANIMALS

Depending on your living situation, you may want to consider investing in working animals. Remember that you will need to maintain and as prep for them as well so plan accordingly if you want to add working animals to your prep.

# Dogs

A good guard dog can work as a deterrent against attackers. Attackers usually prey on easy targets and the presence of an intimidating dog makes you a less attractive target. Usual guard dog breeds include Rottweilers, Dobermans, German Shepherds and Akitas. True to their breeding, any guard dog breed can be aggressive to strangers and need to be properly trained and socialized if you want to take them outside their territory.

After a lot of research, we decided that a livestock guardian dog (LGD) would best suit our needs. The most common LGD breeds in the US are Great Pyrenees, Anatolian Shepherds, Akbash and Maremmas. We settled on a Great Pyrenees/Akbash mix and couldn't be happier. At a full-grown size of 100-120 lbs, these dogs are very formidable creatures. Bred to protect livestock and to patrol farms, LGDs are very intelligent but have a mind of their own.

In the Old World, many of these LGD breeds were also left to fend for themselves and their charges for days on end without the presence of a human keeper. The resulting trait is a resourceful dog with modest food requirements for their size. LGDs work best in rural settings, preferably on larger acreage. They are generally not known to do well in urban or suburban areas.

Make sure that any breed you decide on is suitable for your living situation and complies with the rules and regulations of your domicile. Some breeds may not be allowed by city ordinances, your Home Owner's Association (HOA) rules, or may increase your homeowner's insurance premiums. Some insurers will not insure homeowners with certain dog breeds like Pit Bulls.

Cover your bases before investing in any guard dog breed. You will need to plan for its feeding cost and general care. Prepping for your dog's feeding needs is actually quite easy. According to holistic veterinarian, Dr. Questen (http://drquesten.com), once you have your vet's blessing, you can add home-cooked foods to your pet's diet.

According to Dr. Questen, the amount should generally not be more than 25-50% of their regular diet at first and additional supplements such as egg shell calcium may be needed to make the meal nutritionally complete. Once your pet is used to the new diet, it can consist of 1/3 grains (like rice), 1/3 legumes (like beans, peas or chickpeas) and 1/3 vegetables. These ingredients are fit for human consumption and make for easier food stockpile planning.

# Chickens

Besides having dogs for personal protection, as long as you're able and allowed to keep them, you may also want to consider investing in some food-producing livestock like backyard chickens and/or bees.

I'll admit that chickens lie close to my heart. It was my want of chickens that set me and my family on an unexpected homesteading path. We'd specifically purchased property that would allow for chickens. This property and its location inevitably led us to becoming preppers.

In good times, a few backyard chickens are an excellent way of turning food and kitchen waste into eggs, fertilizer (which needs to be composted for a year before it can be used on plants) and, believe it or not, into entertainment! However, in addition to the cost of feeding your chickens, you will have startup costs like building a coop and possibly a run. The needs for your chickens will vary greatly, depending on your climate, location, the size of your flock, the kinds of predators in the vicinity, what kinds of chicken breeds you have and zoning laws.

Besides providing fresh eggs most of the year, your chickens can be turned into a meat source if needed. If you don't generally consume a lot of eggs, selling your chicken eggs may also be an additional income source. Prices for farm fresh eggs will vary depending on region, with organic, pastured eggs being the most valuable. Make sure that you abide by your state's cottage food laws before you start selling your eggs.

There are many chicken breeds to choose from. If your main concern is egg production, I recommend White Leghorns. For fast meat-only production, breeds like the Cornish-X are a good choice. Rhode Island Reds make a good dual-purpose (both meat and egg production) breed.

If you'd like to read more about keeping chickens when breed choices, I've written two books, "How to Keep Backyard Chickens" and "The Best Backyard Chicken Breeds" (http://byjillb.com), which may help you with your chicken-keeping journey.

## Bee-Keeping

Bees are another prepper livestock to consider if your jurisdiction allows for it. While bees, like chickens, need less maintenance than most other traditional livestock, they still need to be maintained and taken care of. The cost of hives and other bee equipment will run you about $300 for a beginner's kit, plus the cost of the bees.

However, some states or state universities may offer funding for the beginning beekeeper. Virginia, for example, has a Beehive Grant Fund (http://hyperurl.co/vabeegrant) for new beekeepers. Contact your State Apiarist for more information to see what's available in your state.

If you're unable to get funding, you can try to find used equipment from someone who's giving the hobby up. Check Craigslist or your local Beekeepers' Association to see if you can get any leads for getting used equipment. Just make sure that the used equipment hasn't been infected with disease, which can infect your new hive. If you're able, you can try catch your own bee swarm which will be free. However, I don't recommend this route unless you know what you're doing.

With honey bees, you not only have pollinators, which are very important for fruit production, but you also have a renewable source of honey (for both sweetening and medicinal purposes) as well as beeswax (for soap and candle-making).

# 16 Lighting

You will need some kind of lighting in an emergency situation. If you have bees and therefore beeswax, that it probably the best renewable lighting resource that you can produce. While you can also use lard or tallow to make candles, I think these fats are better used for cooking or making soap (in the case of inedible deer tallow).

## Candles

Unless you're producing your own beeswax, it is generally more expensive than other waxes like soy, to buy. If you don't have beeswax but want to make your own candles cheaply, broken crayons are a good source of free soy wax. Good places to get your hands on crayons include schools, day care centers and family restaurants. This colored soy wax and can be melted into candles. The colorants may however, make the flame burn at an indeterminate temperature. Other wax options include palm wax.

The plus side to using beeswax is that it will burn for a few more hours than other waxes. It also has a higher melting point of 144 -147 degrees F, which keeps it in solid form in just about any outdoor condition. However, it cools and hardens very fast and is much harder to clean up. **Do not use good cookware to make your wax candles.** If possible, use pots dedicated to candle-making.

Making your own candles is fairly simple. The process is similar whether you use wax or rendered tallow or lard. **Caution: Candle-making involves working with fire and hot wax/fats and is done at your own risk.**

You will need: your choice of wax, wicks, wick tabs (optional but the tabs will make it easier to set the wicks into the candle) and containers to mold your candles in. The containers can include glass jars, tealight cups or metal tins, as long as it doesn't melt, burn or explode from the heat. If you don't like using containers, you can also mold your candles in clean cardboard milk containers. Just tear the cardboard away after the wax has set, before using.

I don't suggest spending too much on your candle containers. Commercial glass jars will generally work but canning jars are better because they are specifically made to be stronger and to withstand more heat and pressure. Otherwise, metal containers that are not lined can work as well.

You will also need a melting pot or container, a pair of scissors for trimming your wick, and oven mitts or a hot pad to handle your containers with. The best way to melt your wax is to use a double boiler. That is, using a container within a container. For the inner container, you can use an cleaned soup can to melt the wax in. Then place the container with wax in a pot of water, slowly bringing the water to a simmer. Allow the wax to liquefy. Make sure that the water in the double boiler does not dry out or you'll risk having the wax burst into flames.

Next, prepare your candle containers. If the wicks are not primed, you may need to submerge the length of the wick into the melted wax. Once submerged, you should see some air bubbles rise to the surface. Keep the wick submerged for about 2-3 minutes before pulling it out, allowing the excess wax to drip back into the wax container. If the wicks are not pre-tabbed, thread the wicks through the tabs.

Use tweezers to pull both ends of the wick to straighten it out. Lay the stretched primed wick on wax paper and allow it to dry. It should be hard when cool. Cut it to size - about the length of your candle mold plus about three extra inches. Avoid using metal core wicks which burn very hot and smell bad when you put them out.

You can purchase candle-making supplies from Amazon or Nature's Garden (http://naturesgardencandles.com) at reasonable prices. If you want to save even more and make your own wicks, you can use cotton string or twine like "butcher's twine". Process your twine like you would unprimed wicks. I've read that some people drill a hole in pennies and use them as tabs. However, I've never tried this using pennies as tabs and cannot say if it is an easy process or not.

If you want to slow the wick's burn-rate and reduce smoke production, you'll need to dip the wick into a borax solution for 15 minutes. To make the borax solution, mix 2 tablespoons of table salt and 4 tablespoons of borax in 1.5 cups of warm water. Borax is normally used for washing and laundry and can be found in the detergent section of most grocery stores. Allow the dipped wicks/string to dry on a clothesline. Once completely dried, you can prime the wicks in wax as described in the earlier paragraphs.

If you're using glass containers, it is a good idea to warm them up either in the oven, by a stove or even with a hair dryer so that they don't crack from thermal shock when you pour your hot wax in. Position the wick in your candle container. You can loop the wick around a pencil or chopstick positioned on top of your candle container. Once the wick is in place, you can pour the hot wax in. Beeswax hardens quickly. Once filled, immediately but carefully straighten your wick.

The process is the same, regardless of the kind of wax or tallow you use. Make a few of these candles for unexpected power outages but keep most of your supplies on hand rather than pre-making a large number of candles then having to deal with the extra clutter. Tape a book of matches to each jar so that you don't have to fumble in the dark for matches.

Avoid adding scents for survival candles. Many scents can cause headaches or nausea if used in excess and/or for long periods of time. If you plan on reusing the wax, these oils may also not properly remix and may catch on fire or burn someone. Lastly, burning a scented candle is a good way of attracting attention - not a good idea if you are trying to hide.

If you're buying wax, wicks and new 8 oz canning jars for to make your candles, your final cost will be about $1.50-$2 per candle. If you use recycled containers and your own wicks and wax or tallow, the cost will be much lower. Being frugal, make and reuse as much as you can.

If you enjoy making candles, consider turning it into a side business. Etsy or, depending on your location, your local farmer's market, Facebook or Craigslist are all potential places where you can launch your business.

## Other Lighting Sources

Besides making your own candles, it's a good idea to keep other light sources on hand. These can include a small LED keychain flashlight, a larger Everyday Carry (EDC) flashlight and home lighting. For flashlights, the features to consider include type and number of batteries needed, hours of light it provides on low mode, the option of high and low modes, lumens (brightness), weight and size. It should also be impact-resistant and waterproof.

Choose lights that need common sizes like AA or AAA. AAA battery-powered flashlights tend to have a shorter run time as compared to their AA-powered counterparts. Keep things standard by having flashlights that use AA batteries because AAs can power many other items as well.

For home lighting, I like using solar-powered LED lights. In a pinch, you can use solar patio or garden lights that are affordably-priced at clearance when summer ends. Otherwise, having an outdoor LED lantern that is dual-powered by solar or battery is a good idea. I also have a solar/hand-crank flashlight/siren/radio device that can both provide light and some news or entertainment. Choose a model that includes a cellphone charger.

# 17 POWER SOURCES

In the previous chapter on lighting, we start to see the need for batteries. Backup generators are great - as a backup but are not a long-term solution because they have run time limitations. They may also not be practical for apartment dwellers. The noise from a running generator may also attract too much attention in dire grid-down situations. Finally, generators will become useless if the power outage outlasts the fuel supply.

We therefore need to look beyond generators for long-term emergency preparation. Batteries play a big role in our prep and it's a good idea to have a stash of common-sized NiMH rechargeable AA and AAA batteries. Keep other sizes like 9V, Ds and Cs in smaller numbers.

You can recharge your NiMH batteries by plugging them into an appropriate fold-up solar charger. Choose a solar charger with USB-type adapters. Most now include these USB-type adaptors. Otherwise, you'll need to have a car-charger connecting to the solar charger. Smaller 5 or 10-watt solar chargers are suitable for charging cell phones, e-readers, some LED lights, flashlights and even some radios.

If you need to charge a laptop, you'll need 25 to 40-watt solar chargers. For additional wattage power, invest in fold-up chargers that can be linked to other chargers with adapters. Chargers that have a built-in battery will allow you to run some appliances even without sunlight.

Some solar chargers may even have a built in high capacity battery or a small inverter that can power 120-V AC equipment. Although convenient, you will only be able to power small AC appliances with these solar chargers. You'll probably be better off investing in small DC-powered appliances instead of a solar charger with an AC-inverter. DC-powered appliances like portable DVD-players, radios, LED lanterns and even small fridges are sold at RV or boating supply stores.

I admit that there the endless number of solar charging options can almost be paralyzing. Like all the other preps in this book, there is no one "true" way, only the way that works best for you. I've included a list of solar charging options in the Appendix to help to start you off. The recommendations are by Jeff Yago, P.E., CEM in his Backwoods Home Magazine article.

# 18 ENTERTAINMENT

It never hurts to lighten things up especially when times are tough. If you have kids, stock up on paper, pencils, crayons and other craft supplies. These items normally go on sale at office supply and big-box stores before the back-to-school season. For details on how to snag the best deals, please refer to "The Modern American Frugal Housewife Book #3 - Moms Edition" (http://byjillb.com).

Other items may include playing cards, board games, puzzles and books. Make it known that you're looking for board games. We've been gifted games from unexpected places, including our local Resource Center.

With regards to books, I like e-readers. Instead of trying to store a library of print books, a back-lit e-reader can store around 800-2,500 books on a small device. The actual number of books you'll be able to store will depend on the device's memory and book file size. I admit that when I first heard about e-readers sometime back in 2007, I thought that it was the most ridiculous thing.

Then, because gone are the days of the free toaster, I received a free Kindle when I opened a new bank account and became a convert! I've since downloaded more free or very cheap books that I can probably ever read. E-readers currently costs as little as $50 so investing in one is almost a no-brainer.

# 19 COMMUNITY

Last but not least, the ultimate prep is developing community. Love and belonging sit on the upper tiers of Maslow's Hierarchy of Needs but may turn out to be one of the most important things you can do for your prep. So many survivalists discuss "hunkering down" in their little underground bunker or setting themselves up in some isolated location but I don't think this is a realistic idea of prepping.

Fact is, we simply can't do everything alone. We need a community to survive and thrive when times are good. We need a community even more when times are bad. Reach out to your neighbors. They'll be the ones closest in proximity to you.

Perhaps you can start pooling your resources now by starting a bulk food purchasing co-op or planning your food gardens together so that you can swap different crops. Now is a good time to figure out who is reliable and who isn't. If you can't rely on someone now, there's a very good chance that you won't be able to rely on them when things crumble.

On a larger level, work towards making your community more resilient. Push for community food gardens. In World War II, people planted Victory Gardens in the US, Canada, the UK, Australia and even in Germany to help to defend the community's food supply.

On the flipside, when the Japanese occupied Malaya and my home country of Singapore in World War II, they tried to encourage the populus to grow food in any available place to help to combat inflation. The campaign was a failure despite increasing Japanese penalties for not complying. The majority of the population was unwilling to take part in the program because they believed that the British would return to the colony soon and that things would return to normal. Malnutrition ensued.

The locals who did turn to growing food had no knowledge of farming and quickly depleted soil fertility with intensive farming practices. Instead of composting as recommended by the Japanese occupying forces, the population turned to the traditional Chinese method of fertilizing with human excrement with dire results - diseases from typhoid to cholera spread.

## 20 CONCLUSION

Don't let bad history repeat itself in *your* community. The current highly centralized and monolithic US agricultural system is a fragile one. We don't need terrorists or occupying forces to take the food system down. It can take itself down by its own doing, be it from resource depletion (like peak oil), unexpected ecological consequences of GMOs etc (which echos to Mao's Great Leap Forward campaign), agri-corporate meltdown (mismanagement), or natural agricultural disasters (as in the Irish potato famine).

We can make ourselves more resilient if we prepare. Trying to tackle so many things at once may be intimidating but it doesn't have to be if you take it a step at a time. Diversify. If you don't know how to cook, start slow by cooking dried spaghetti and serve it with commercially prepared sauce. Work your way up to making hearty soups. Tend to of a pot of herbs. Grow a tomato plant from seed. Break bread with others. You'll be happier and healthier doing all these things and you'll prepare for the worst with less fear.

**Sign up for book updates at http://byjillb.com.**

**Disclaimer & Disclosure:** This guide is for entertainment and informational purposes only. The author and anyone associated with this book shall not be held liable for damages incurred through the use of information provided herein. Content included on this book is not intended to be, nor does it constitute, the giving of financial, legal or professional advice.

The author and others associated with this book make no representation as to the accuracy, completeness or validity of any information in this book. While every caution has been taken to provide the most accurate information, please use your own discretion before making any decisions based solely on the content herein. The author and others associated with this book are not liable for any errors or omissions nor will provide any form of compensation if you suffer an inconvenience, loss or damages of any kind because of, or by making use of, the information contained herein. Any opinion given is the author's own, based on her experience. If in doubt, always seek the advice of a professional who can advise you appropriately before acting on any part of this book.

This book contains references and links to other Third Party products and services. Some of these references have been included for the convenience of the readers and to make the book more complete. They should not be construed as endorsements from, or of any of these Third Parties or their products or services. These links and references may contain products and opinions expressed by their respective owners. The author does not assume liability or responsibility for any Third Party material or opinions. Links denoted by an asterisk (*) may contain affiliate links for which the author may receive compensation for click-through purchases.

RESOURCES

## Water Storage

Waterbob http://waterbob.com

## Canning Recipe Sources

"So Easy to Preserve" by the USDA and The University of Georgia
"Ball Complete Book of Home Preserving"
University of Oregon Extension
http://extension.oregonstate.edu/fch/food-preservation
University of Alaska Extension (metal canning)
http://hyperurl.co/uafcan

## Food Sources

The Church of Latter-Day Saints (LDS)
http://hyperurl.co/ldsmre
Emergency Essentials http://beprepared.com
Golden Organics http://goldenorganics.net
Honeyville, Inc http://honeyville.com/
The Ready Store http://www.thereadystore.com/mre

## Food Grade Diatomaceous Earth

Custom Milling http://bit.ly/1wpjwCx
Perma-Guard http://bit.ly/1xjm8oi

## Seeds

Baker Creek Heirloom Seeds http://rareseeds.com
Bountiful Gardens http://www.bountifulgardens.org
Johnny's Selected Seeds http://www.johnnyseeds.com/
Seed Savers Exchange http://www.seedsavers.org/
Southern Exposure Seed Exchange
http://www.southernexposure.com/
Sustainable Seed Company http://sustainableseedco.com
Victory Seed Company http://www.victoryseeds.com

## Off-Grid Living Goods

Candle-Making Supplies http://naturesgardencandles.com
Lehman's http://lehmans.com

## DIY Links

DIY Charcoal http://www.pine3.info/Charmake.htm
DIY Wonder Oven http://hyperurl.co/sewwonderoven
DIY Solar Cooker Plans http://solarcooking.org/plans/
DIY Solar Dehydrator Plans http://hyperurl.co/solardiy
Diaper Patterns http://hyperurl.co/diaperpatterns
Menstrual Pad Patterns http://hyperurl.co/freepadpattern
How to Fold a Diaper http://hyperurl.co/folddiaper
Soap Calculator  http://bit.ly/1AB4KB6

APPENDIX

## Optional Starter Carpentry Tools

Assorted nails, bolts, nuts and screws
12/16/21 ounce claw hammers
Wrenches and socket set
Hacksaw and blades
Chalkline
Water level
Nail pullers
Rip saw
Cross cut saw
Carpenter's square
Staple gun and staples
8" and 12" levels
Miter box and saw
Countersink
Hand drill and bit selection
Screwdriver set
Calipers
Sharpening tools

## Optional Starter Wood-Splitting Tools
Hand saw
Cross-cut saw
Chain-saw and extra parts
Sledgehammer
Splitting maul
Splitting wedges
Axes

## Optional Starter Gardening Tools

Various shovels
Digging forks
Buckets
Hoes
Trowels
Watering cans
Wheel cultivators

## Solar Chargers

### Smaller Chargers
Enerplex http://www.goenerplex.com
Endless Sun Solar http://www.endlesssunsolar.com
P3Solar http://www.p3solar.com
Secur http://www.securproducts.com
Suntactics http://www.suntactics.com

### Larger Chargers
Aspect Solar http://www.aspectsolar.com
Goal Zero http://www.goalzero.com
Strongvolt http://www.strongvolt.com
Sunjack http://www.sunjack.com
Sun Ready Power http://www.sunreadypower.com
Sol Pro http://www.solpro.com

BIBLIOGRAPHY AND REFERENCES

*Ask Jackie: Food Storage*, Jackie Clay (Backwoods Home Magazine, 2012)
*Baking Soda Bonanza*, Peter A. Ciullo (HarperCollins, 2009)
Backwoods Home Magazine
http://www.comfyclothpads.com
http://www.countryfarm-lifestyles.com
*Mrs Owen's Beginning Prepper Guide For Women: Looking To The Future With Joy*, Katie Owens
Missouri Department of Conservation (http://hyperurl.co/modeer)
http://www.endtimesreport.com
EPA Office of Water 4606-M (EPA 816-F-15-003) June 2015
Hillbilly Housewife (http://hillbillyhousewife.com)
http://www.pine3.info/Charmake.htm
Surviving in Argentina (http://ferfal.blogspot.com)
Singapore National Library Board (http://eresources.nlb.gov.sg)
http://survivalistprepper.net
http://thebugoutbagguide.com
*The Gift of Fear and Other Survival Signals that Protect Us From Violence*, Gavin de Becker (Dell, 1999)
http://www.teotwawki-blog.com
LA Times (http://hyperurl.co/castironcare)

## Books By Jill b.

Please check out my other books at
**http://byjillb.com**:

### The Modern Frugal American Housewife Book #1
*Home Economics*

### The Modern Frugal American Housewife Book #2
*Organic Gardening*

### The Modern Frugal American Housewife Book #3
*Moms Edition*

### The Modern Frugal American Housewife Book #4
*Emergency Prepping*

### CAN Dos and Don'ts
*Water Bath and Pressure Canning*

### How to Keep Backyard Chickens
*A Straightforward Beginner's Guide*

### The Best Backyard Chicken Breeds
*A List of Top Birds for Pets, Eggs and Meat*

### Foraging
*A Beginner's Guide to Wild Edible and Medicinal Plants*

### Medicinal Herb Gardening
*10 Plants for The Self-Reliant Homestead Prepper*

## How to Make Money on eBay: Beginner's Guide

*From Setting Up Accounts to Selling Like a Pro*

## How to Make Money on eBay: Maximize Profits

*Secrets, Stories, Tips and Hacks - Confessions of a 16-Year eBay Veteran*

## How to Make Money on eBay: International Sales

*Taking the Fear and Guesswork Out of Doing Business Internationally on eBay*

## Self-Publishing on a Budget with Amazon

*A Guide for the Author Publishing eBooks on Kindle*

# ABOUT THE AUTHOR

HomeGrown • HomeMade • HomeBusiness • HOMESTEAD

Jill b. is an author, entrepreneur, homesteader and is the co-inventor and co-founder of Chicken Armor (http://chickenarmor.com), an affordable, low maintenance chicken saddle. She has also written over a dozen homesteading and home business books.

With a no-nonsense style, Jill draws from her own experiences and mistakes, and writes books focusing on maximizing output with minimal input to save you time and money.

Jill has been mentioned/quoted in various publications including The Associated Press, The New York Times, The Denver Post and ABC News. She has written for various magazines including Countryside and Small Stock Journal, Molly Green, Farm Show Magazine and Backyard Poultry Magazine. She holds an Engineering degree from an Ivy League from a previous life.

At its height, her homestead included over 100 chickens, geese and ducks, as well as cats, a dog, bees and a donkey named Elvis. She currently lives on her homestead in rural Oregon.

Learn more by visiting her site http://byjillb.com.

www.ingramcontent.com/pod-product-compliance
Lightning Source LLC
Chambersburg PA
CBHW020539290526
45786CB00002B/953

9 781530 111947